Praise for *The Game*

'Any of us who write about spor this kind of book at some point. A explain it (and us), to stake its oute ..... in our own peculiar way. Thankfully for all concerned, Tadhg Coakley has saved the world the bother of having to plough through all that. *The Game* is a thoughtful, artful gem.'

Malachy Clerkin

'A heartfelt exploration of sport and so much more. A many-chambered book that is empathetic and engaging.'

Sinéad Gleeson

'This is a towering work. ... The essays 'Miracles' and 'Kisses' are two of the most beautiful, poignant and heartfelt pieces of writing I've ever read.

'Tadhg is clear-eyed, intelligent, and unrelentingly honest about the darkness that pervades the business of sport and its capacity to arouse our basest instincts ... He asks the hardest of questions and delivers unflinchingly honest answers. This is no paean ... it is a brilliantly forensic and startlingly objective account of the ways that sport at once transcends, debases and delineates our humanity.

'Tadhg admits to feeling like an outsider but he is firmly and undeniably in the inner circle of the great sportswriters. And he is clearly, though he'd probably deny it, the truest of sportsmen.'

Donal Ryan

Tadhg Coakley's debut novel *The First Sunday in September* hinged around a fictional All-Ireland hurling final and was published in 2018 to much acclaim. His second offering, *Whatever It Takes*, was chosen as the 2020 Cork, One City One Book. Coakley's writing has been published in *The Stinging Fly*, *Winter Papers*, The42 and *The Irish Times*, and he writes about sport for the *Irish Examiner*.

Also by Tadhg Coakley

The First Sunday in September

Whatever It Takes

Everything, the Autobiography of Denis Coughlan

THE
GAME

A JOURNEY INTO
THE HEART OF SPORT

TADHG COAKLEY

MERRION
PRESS

First published in 2022 by
Merrion Press
10 George's Street
Newbridge
Co. Kildare
www.merrionpress.ie

9781785372971 (Paper)
9781785372988 (Ebook)

A CIP catalogue record for this book is available from the British Library.

Typeset in Adobe Caslon Pro by riverdesignbooks.com

Front cover image: Author on Banna Strand, Co. Kerry, taken by Dermot Coakley.

Merrion Press is a member of Publishing Ireland.

*In memory of
my mother and father:
Kitty and Tim Coakley*

'Thanks for the day, for everything. It would have crowned it had they won,' I said as we parted.

'What's it but a game? We had the day. Thanks yourself for coming all the way over.' James waved, and I saw him wait at the gate until I passed out of sight behind the alders along the shore.

– 'Love of the World', John McGahern

PREFACE

I attended a reading by my one of my favourite writers, Elizabeth Strout, at the Borris House Festival of Writing & Ideas in June 2018. When Sinéad Gleeson asked her if she would write a memoir, Elizabeth said no, that in her fiction she was hiding behind her characters and she wanted to stay there and never expose herself in the light.

I realised at that moment I was going to write this book.

I had just written a novel in stories, *The First Sunday in September*, about a fictional All-Ireland hurling final Sunday and how eighteen people interacted with the day and its sport. After hearing Elizabeth, I realised I was hiding behind the characters in my novel, describing my intimacies with sport and my perspectives on sport through their eyes and in their voices.

But, unlike Elizabeth Strout, I was willing – more, I needed – to expose myself and make clear to readers my relationships with sport and what they mean to me and why. And through me, what sport means to all of us.

Why in 2019 did 46 per cent of Ireland's adult population – 1.7 million people – participate regularly in sport (through volunteering, attending sports events or being a member of a sports club), almost evenly split across genders? Why does the GAA have 2,600 clubs worldwide with over 500,000 members? Why do 93 per cent of people in India (1.28 billion souls) self-identify as sports fans? Why do 70 per cent of people in the USA follow sport and devote an average of 7.7 hours a week to it? Why, in 2016, was sport a $500 billion industry in the United States and valued worldwide at $1.3 trillion? Why are cemeteries all across Ireland decked out in county and club colours before championship finals? Why were 'European Championship' and 'Premier League' the most searched terms in Google in Ireland in 2021 and why were Christian Eriksen and Gordon Elliott the most searched names? Why did 90,000 Limerick women, men and children come out to greet their victorious hurlers in 2018? And what will be the turnout for the Mayo footballers, when they bring home Sam Maguire?

Why are so many people we know and love so interested in sport?

In this book, I'm trying to answer these questions, partly by exploring my own experiences in sport and partly by using the cultural discourse of those who have thought about sport before me.

The book is not a paean to sport. In it I confront the dark passions aroused by sport, its political exploitation, its excesses and a deep-grained sexism at its core. I do this by also challenging my own behaviour.

The prospect of coming out from behind my fictional characters was terrifying and is terrifying, and the writing of this book was – at times – a painful uncovering of my life.

But I hope you will see your life in this book, too, and other lives lit up by sport.

I hope you will see what sport says about emotion, identity, initiation, memory, family, the miraculous, the collective, art, toxic masculinity, corruption, sexism, addiction, loss, recovery, ecstasy, the body, masculinity, joy and innocence.

And love.

Especially love.

Tadhg Coakley
April 2022

CONTENTS

PART 1

THE GAME

I USED TO PLAY A FOOTBALL GAME I devised at my home on the Cork Road, Mallow. I may have been eleven or twelve. It was before I went to boarding school, and I was still innocent and cheerful, so I must have been twelve and the year must have been 1973. Let's go with that.

It was a solo game and the idea was to kick the ball around the house in the least possible number of touches. It began on the path near the top of our back garden and it ended by kicking the ball into our dog Faust's kennel, again in the back garden. A clockwise loop.

We lived in a moderately sized bungalow, built in the late 1940s (around the time my mother and father got married) in a suburban part of the town. My parents had built extensions at the back and front of the house in the 1960s, making for tight spaces and many corners, which didn't make my task of guiding the ball all the way around any easier.

I imagine it as sunny, but not really hot – partial cloud, let's say. It's summer. And I'm alone. Somehow my younger brother and sister, Padraig and Pauline, are inside the house with my mother (or they have all gone to the shop, maybe). My eldest sister Mary has probably moved away from home by now. Úna and Cathy might be at work – we all worked during the summer holidays when we were old enough. Perhaps this was the summer my two older brothers, Dermot and John, went to New York City. My father is definitely at work.

Faust, our red setter, isn't around either – which is strange, he wouldn't be inside and if he were outside, he would bother me, chasing the ball or interfering with key moments in the game. But it's important that I'm on my own for this – my memory demands it.

I'm wearing bell-bottom trousers (this being the 1970s) and white runners (what we called 'rubber dollies' those days) and a short-sleeved shirt with big collars (the style of the time). I'm small and thin and healthy and fair (with longish hair). I'm fit and I love being outside, playing football (which some people call soccer) or hurling. I love to move. Movement is living for me when I'm twelve and I'm very good at it.

Luckily for me, sport is all about movement too, about grace under pressure. Which, when you see it at the very highest level – in, say, Roger Federer or Simone Biles – elevates the bringer of that movement to a state of 'being both flesh and not', something human but also otherworldly. This is how David Foster Wallace would later describe Federer.

The first kick is from under the Lawson cypress trees near the top of our back garden, towards the house. It's down the concrete path that dissects the garden – a long shot, maybe thirty yards – with a very small target at the end, a gap of only three feet or so, between the two pillars of my mother's ornate garden wall. Slightly downhill. A lawn on my left and beds of vegetables on my right.

This kick takes skill, but I had skill with a football then. You have to hit the ball with a precise part of the foot (the left foot in my case), somewhere between the instep and the side of the foot. Too much of the instep and the ball could veer to the left; too much of the side of the foot and the ball could meander off to the right. The ball must rise from the ground in its first motion, but only slightly. Then it skips a couple of times, childlike, and then it rolls to its target: the back wall of the house outside our living room (what we called the New Room).

I kick the ball towards the gap in the wall. Not too hard and not too soft, just the right shade of firm. That's the way for accuracy when passing a ball, which is essentially what I am doing. I am honing skills that I will use in a few years' time for my local team, Mallow United. I am also developing the rigour and discipline I will later use in other sports.

Of course I didn't know that I was honing skills or building rigour when I was playing this game, I thought I was just playing with a ball.

I also didn't know that in this game I was preparing myself for all the agonies and ecstasies that sport would grant me for the rest of my life.

The second shot I have to take is very delicate. I have to lob the ball over my mother's garden wall and out through the doorway by the garage to my left. This is achieved by placing the toe of the foot under the ball and pushing hard and upwards – more of a nudge than a kick or a shot.

I have to use this technique to get the ball very high very quickly over the wall, which is quite close by, but it's technically difficult to control. For starters, the ball has to be stopped or moving very slowly, unlike when kicking. It's harder to be accurate laterally and to control the height and distance – football is a three-dimensional game, don't forget. If I don't get enough height, I'll hit the wall and it'll cost me at least two more touches. If I go left, the ball will end up in my mother's dahlias and sweet peas – again a minimum two penalty count (and the guilt of breaking my mother's lovely flowers). If I'm too high, I might hit the electricity wire or the beam across the top of the doorway. If I go right I'll hit my brothers' bedroom wall – a touch lost.

But if I do it right, the ball will end up on our driveway, which slopes down past the front of the house to the Cork Road, and its momentum will bring it all the way to the ideal spot for the next shot.

I lob the ball over the wall and through the doorway. I walk out after it. On the left of the drive is an old hedge between us and our neighbours, the Noonans, but it won't snag the ball, so it doesn't matter. On the right is the pebble-dashed flank of the house, so the ball will swan its meandering way to where I will take my third touch. (Unless there is a car in the drive, which will require another touch to go around it – but, guess what: there isn't a car; my mother has kindly gone for her messages to Sexton's or into town.)

For my next touch, the third, I have to get the pace just right. But I've plenty of time to steady myself as my ball and I amble together down the drive. And I've done this hundreds of times before.

It's a rough tarmac drive, stones embedded in the asphalt, except at the top near the garage, which is concrete. I'm just walking with my ball down the gentle slope. Past the kitchen window. Past the sash window of the bedroom I share with Padraig. On down to the long, narrow extension at the front, which we called the front hall. That has glass all the way round (not football-friendly for boisterous matches in the front lawn).

Cars pass, at speed, on the road at the end of the drive, but I'm not aware of them.

My target is the front lawn of the house, through a narrow gap between a stone pillar and the corner of the front hall. I know my line and the pace I need. I must angle the ball away from the front of the house because there are steps up to the front door and it's a disaster if I hit those – an inexcusable, unforced error. I take the shot and it's fine.

Now I'm on the front lawn – halfway around my loop. For my fourth kick I have to bend the ball so that it swings low around the front of the porch and spins up the other side of the house along the narrow path between its gable end and the hedge separating us from our other neighbours, the Curtins. I have to do this with the inside of my left foot and I have to hit the ball really hard. If I get it just right (and in this telling of my game, I do) the ball will ricochet off the concrete of a triangular kerb at the top of the path and come to a stop outside our back door. I take the shot and race up the side of the house after it.

I'm standing by the stationary ball, facing the narrow path towards our back garden. The window of my sisters' bedroom is behind me. On my immediate right the back door with its clear Perspex panels. Above me the sound of starlings who have nested inside the rotting soffit and make a racket as well as a mess on the ground. My mother has trained a passion flower to spread around this space and the delicate and beautiful Daliesque blossoms surround me, heavy with their religious symbolism.

Ahead, on my left, our two old sheds, comprising a long low building with a corrugated asbestos roof. The first one contains old paint, bits and pieces of bulky waste, wellington boots, a table, a gas cooker (in case the electric one in the kitchen fails – or in addition to it at Christmas) and sometimes vegetables from the garden. The second shed is full of blocks and coal, fuel for the fire in winter. It also sticks out about a foot from the other shed, making the target for my shot even narrower.

On my right the waste pipes and drains of two toilets that were built as part of the extension. These don't interfere with my kick (they're too close to me), but – further on – the chimney breast of the New Room sticks out and has snagged many the shot. Between the chimney breast and the second shed, there's only a foot and a half of passageway and it's maybe ten yards away. The ball has to thread this needle. I take the shot.

For my sixth touch I have to chip the ball over the garden wall on to the back lawn. This wall seems strange to me now. In hindsight, I'm surprised my mother allowed it because it's a bit too fancy for her. It is narrow and about four feet high, with a curved top. It is comprised of thin concrete bricks, each with several holes fanning out around a central circular piece. Underneath there is a concrete base because the garden is a bit higher than the path.

On my left a small piece of garden where we had a compost heap. On my right the corner of the New Room, stippled with pebble-dash. I rest my hand against the wall and feel its rough familiarity. I chip the ball over the wall and onto the back lawn.

I walk past the New Room window and turn left into the back garden. No rush, now. For my last shot I have to direct the ball into Faust's kennel, which is by Noonans' hedge. It's a small target, less than two feet across and about three feet high.

I walk to the ball. I take three steps back. I look at the ball and the kennel for a long time. I step forward, right foot first, then left; then I carefully plant my right foot down beside the ball. Before my right foot has grounded itself I'm already moving my left foot towards the ball. My head is down, my eyes are locked on, my right arm is raised, my body is slightly angled.

There I am: a happy, innocent boy standing in my back garden, my whole life ahead of me, playing a game with a ball. Around me, my childhood home and my family: safe, fulfilled, intact.

On either side of our house and garden, the homes of our neighbours, the Noonans and the Curtins and the homes of our friends on Cork Road and in Dromore Drive. The tarmac road outside Redmonds' and Endersons' where I will play football with my friends. The Back Field behind, where I will play hurling and football with my friends and my Mallow teammates. The Mallow Town Park across the Blackwater river where I will play football and hurling and Gaelic football as a boy and as a man. Carhookeal on the Old Cork Road and the big complex in Carrigoon to the east to where the GAA club will migrate. Mallow Golf Club, across the river from Carrigoon, where, later, I will be a member for years and play many happy rounds.

All the other pitches I will play on, in Buttevant and Fermoy and Cork city and Limerick and Thurles and Dublin. All the pitches and sports grounds I will travel to. Croke Park, Old Trafford, Yankee Stadium, San Siro. The golf courses I will play on, in Mallow, Doneraile and Charleville and all over Cork and Kerry and Waterford and the whole of Ireland. Golf courses in Scotland and Spain and Portugal, in the USA and Canada and New Zealand. All the stadiums and sports grounds I will see on TV. All the pitches and the courses and the race tracks and the courts around the world, now and always – stretching out in space and time. Wherever children or adults have played, are playing now, or will ever play sport.

I take the shot.

EKSTASIS

YOU ARE IN CAPPOQUIN, ON THE St Colman's College Under 14½ Gaelic football team in a Munster Final against Dungarvan CBS. Your team is narrowly losing with a few minutes to go. Your trainer, Father Jackie Corkery, shouts: 'Coakley, go in centre forward.' He means Gerry Coakley from Aghinagh, but Gerry doesn't hear him and you do, so you go in centre forward. You get the ball straight away but are thrown off balance in a tackle and you drop it and hit it on the half-volley. Amazingly, the ball stays low and straight and skids into the bottom corner of the goal. You are filled with the realisation of the ball going in. The knowledge consumes you. All sound is immediately dulled behind some hum – the muffled shouts of your teammates, the groans of the opposition. One Dungarvan player soundlessly curses you to your face. It is like you are underwater. There is the slowness of time, the intensity of disbelief, of *is this happening?* Then the final whistle and a kind of mayhem, you there and not there, inside and outside that time, watching the scene rather than being in it, not taking anything in, not having a clue what is going on at all.

▲▲▲

You are on a Cork Under-16 hurling development team playing against Kerry in Ballyheigue. It is mid-winter and freezing cold and early in the game snow begins to fall, in that silent, busy, fast, slow, dreamlike way that snow has of just coming and coming and blurring the air and sticking to the wet, dumb ground. You and the other hurlers play on in the quiet whiteness and the normal sounds – the slap of a sliotar into a hand, the 'pock' of a hurley hitting the ball, the crack of hurley on hurley, the call of a player or a mentor – the normal sounds are not normal, but strange, heightened and otherworldly. You are subdued by the eeriness that has descended – boys giving their all in their county jerseys, hurling in the snow – the ball hard and unyielding, your hurleys rigid and strange in your perished hands, your chests heaving, your breaths misting, the goals dimming to distance in the falling snow. Your hair and faces and jerseys softly spiked with it. The snow becoming part of the game, falling faintly, faintly falling as Joyce wrote, as you run around in the whiteness, hurling; the stamp of your boots making a slight creaking crunching sound at the edges of the immeasurable white pitch.

▲▲▲

You are eighteen and playing for Cork in the Munster Minor hurling final against Limerick. The game is in its closing moments and the Semple Stadium crowd is swollen to almost 48,000 with the imminence of the Senior game. The ball breaks for you, hopping nicely, about twenty-five yards out, and you meet it perfectly, first time, right-handed, and it tears into the top left corner of the goal. When the boom of the crowd strikes you – literally strikes you – you have a sensation of being both inside and outside your body, and the blood in your head churns and casts you into a dizzying trance, and you can't hear what people are saying to you until after the team returns to the calm of the dressing room.

▲▲▲

You're watching the Wimbledon Final between John McEnroe and Björn Borg. It is 4 July 1981 and you are twenty years old. You're looking at the match in silence in the living room of your house on the Cork Road. Your father is asleep in another chair. He has turned the sound down and you don't dare turn it up again in case he wakes and wants to change the channel. As you arrive, Borg is serving. He is 5–4 down in the fourth set and he needs to win the game to stay in the match. The grass on Centre Court is parched. McEnroe wears a red headband under his long, curly hair. He is tall and thin. He plays in silence. Borg wears a blue and white headband under long straight hair. He is tall and thin. He plays in silence. Borg is trying to win his sixth consecutive Wimbledon title and complete a forty-two consecutive match-winning run in the tournament. In the 1980 Final (the previous year) – long considered to have been the greatest tennis match in history – Borg had beaten McEnroe. You want McEnroe to win, so badly. It's all you crave. He is everything you adore and cannot be: anti-establishment, iconoclastic, fiery, rebellious, arrogant, noisy, inconsiderate, virtuoso. He breaks Borg's serve and drops to his knees in silence. You rise to your feet and punch the mute air. You leave the room, closing the door quietly behind you. You go into your bedroom and sit on the bed and look out the window. You just sit there, looking out the window, in the silence.

▲▲▲

You're playing football for Mallow United, down the Town Park. There's a big home crowd cheering the team on only a few feet from the sideline. It's a must-win top-of-the-league game against St Mary's, your big rivals. You're playing midfield, up against their best player, Martin O'Sullivan, who's heading to the League of Ireland at the end of the season. In the first half he gets the ball and powers towards the Mallow goal. You track back and chase him down. Somehow, you slide in and hook your right foot around the football and win possession, then pivot to put your body between him and the ball. He drags you down. The crowd bellows outrage and then approval as the referee blows for a free kick. You jump up and run back towards the halfway line. 'You fucking good thing, Coakley,' Daniel O'Callaghan, your teammate, says, running beside you. 'Ah come on, Martin!' the St Mary's coach shouts. 'Don't let him do that.' You breathe deeply. You have this. You're better than him. You know this. You can do anything. Anything you want. The winning of the game is yours. Mallow will win and you will make this happen – nothing has ever been more certain in your life. You will do this. You.

▲▲▲

The 1983 Fitzgibbon Cup semi-final on an Ulster University campus pitch in Coleraine. February. Beside the pitch, the River Bann is flowing slow, wide and grey, near where it enters the sea. There is a gale-force wind blowing against UCC and the ball is hit far over the heads of you and your marker. It is near the end of a tough, tight game; you and he are both exhausted. You are corner forward but you are a long way out from the goal, near the sideline. As you both turn and race each other to chase down the ball you feel the presence of a huge ship – it is massive – thrumming its way through the water beside the pitch. It is towering over you, high and dark-hulled. It is as long as the pitch or even longer, it seems never-ending. You and your marker, your teams and the game and the pitch are dwarfed by the ship, by its immensity. You remember nothing about that game except that ship and that moment – not a single thing, not even whom you beat.

▲▲▲

You are being presented with the Fitzgibbon Cup after the 1983 final in Bellaghy. You are captain of the winning UCC team. A small group of you and your teammates stand behind the drab dressing rooms, off to one side, on a little mound of grass, well out of the way of the pitch where Dublin and Derry are playing a Senior Gaelic football National League match. A British army helicopter hovers overhead, but you are so deep in the moment that its din doesn't register. When the official presents you with the cup you almost drop it. You can't see or hear or feel your way out of the place you've gone, or make a speech, or thank your teammates or your mentors or anybody else. You hold the cup in your hands. Standing there, you just look at it.

▲▲▲

It is your last championship hurling game for Mallow, in 1991, against Midleton in Castlelyons. It's early in the summer and you are the captain of the team. The game is drifting into loss, Mallow are four points down, but you are desperate for that not to happen. If you are beaten, the summer of hurling is over – all hurling is over. You can't lose. You can't. You make a frantic effort to score a goal, the ball just managing to worm itself into the corner. Now you will score again, now you will finish the comeback. Moments later, the man marking you turns and puts out his hand for you to shake. 'What?' you say. 'What's happening?' He looks at you strangely. 'It's over, Tadhg,' he says. 'He blew it up.' Another Midleton player approaches you. He says: 'Hard luck.' He looks at you strangely, too. You shake hands with him. You have no idea what is happening. All the players are walking off the pitch. You have no idea what is happening.

▲▲▲

10 September 2013. You're standing on the first tee at Royal Troon in Scotland with Padraig, Brian and Scally. Yesterday it was Kintyre and tomorrow it's Turnberry. Today the wonderful Troon. It's sunny and warm. The famous old granite clubhouse stands proud to your left. You address the ball, take a deep breath and slow everything down. This fairway is a mile wide. You've done this a thousand times. There's a nice breeze in your favour. You slowly draw back the 3-wood and swing as easily as you can manage, trying to keep your head still. The ball flies low and hard up the right side of the fairway, into the light rough. Padraig steps up. He drives it, bang, right down the middle. Brian steps up. Scally makes a joke and you all bend over laughing. Brian drives the ball high and long, straight down the middle. Scally drives it up the left side, and the ball curls back onto the fairway, nice as you like – his natural swing. Brian makes a joke and everybody smiles again. You look around you as you walk towards your golf trolley and try to take it all in. This bliss. The gift of this moment, with such a brother and such friends. All this. How is it possible to be so lucky? How can you prevent yourself from crying with joy?

▲▲▲

The All-Ireland hurling semi-final between Cork and Limerick in Croke Park. 29 July 2018. There has been a sense of unreality in the wash of your emotions all day. The water on Smerwick Harbour a slate grey, waves flecking the surface as you drive past Mount Brandon on your way to Farranfore. A swell of anticipation in the airport, a feeling of belonging, of being among your own. Ease and comfort on the plane; disbelief to be outside a sun-scrubbed Dublin Airport at 10 a.m., when moments before you were passing through Milltown and Firies. Envy, perhaps loss, when overhearing a father and son's intimate conversation on the bus into town. A sense of being blessed, privileged, to be walking in O'Connell Street as the Cork and Limerick fans stroll past the multicultural mix that is Dublin these days. Well-being, rightness. A returning, a catching up with old friends over pints – the feeling of identity, of ritual. With Ray, Michael and Kieran in the Palace Bar on Fleet Street. A kind of joy, not hindered by the porter, while the conversation interlaces itself around you, as natural and full of grace as bird flight. 'Sean South' breaks out from inside the back room – the Limerick lads have begun early. At the old call of the music your emotions shift from your chest to your gut and swell there. There, from an older place, you can reach outward as well as inward, backwards and forwards. You're charged, heightened, more than yourself. You can see everything, and everything is beautiful.

▲▲▲

You are standing outside Páidí Ó Sé's pub, in Ventry. You are trying to reclaim your place in the here and now, after ninety minutes of being subsumed inside the torrid 2019 All-Ireland hurling semi-final between Tipperary and Wexford. Sand martins weave a dreamy thread of air above your head. A benign sun eases away the dark passionate intensity of the match. When Séamus Callanan scored his transcendent goal after ten minutes of the game – delaying and delaying and delaying the hit until the ball was at the apex of its third bounce – you felt your breath catch and your heart lose purchase and your ears buzz and you had to put a hand on the bar counter and steady yourself. From that moment until this one you have been lost inside the game, its power like a black hole's gravitational pull. Now, another version of reality tries to seep back in, under the sky and the sun and the sand martins. You breathe. You walk down to the beach to feel sand between your toes and the breeze in your face. There's a regatta below in *Ceann Trá*. The water of the bay is glinting azure. Iveragh is rising to the south, beyond. You close your eyes and listen to children shrieking joyfully in the water. You turn and walk back the way you came. Fuchsia and foxgloves and purple loosestrife and montbretia and bindweed are flowering on the sides of the road. You walk towards *Cruach Mhárthain* under a West Kerry evening sun, towards home.

PART 2

MIRACLES

I T'S 30 SEPTEMBER 2012. I'M WALKING out of the grounds of Medinah Country Club, about thirty-five miles northwest of Chicago, alongside 40,000 or so other attendees at the final day of the Ryder Cup.

Dusk comes early here, the light is disappearing fast out of a big Illinois sky. The air is growing chill.

I've just been part of the so-called 'Miracle at Medinah'. This is perhaps the greatest comeback in sporting history – definitely in golfing history – when the European Ryder Cup team, against all odds and all predictions, managed to transmute defeat into a dreamlike victory against the red-hot Americans.

The neurotransmitter dopamine is spiking in my brain. My breathing is heavy, dragging in the oxygen I need to fuel my heart's pumping. My mouth is dry. My mind cannot process the unfeasibility of what I've just experienced. There is too much magic to take in.

I'm thinking about my mother. I see her watching the highlights on television at home in Mallow, in the living room of our house on the Cork Road. She was a tidy golfer in her day, winning captains' prizes and presidents' prizes.

She's knitting a pretty sky-blue cardigan for my seven-year-old daughter Roisín. Mammy looks at the telly and smiles. She loves to watch the golf and knit; she finds it soothing. She loves the green of the course and the neatness of the players and the precision and power of their play. The order of it all, the rightness. As a former player she knows the game too, she's intimate with it.

I'm in the midst of a throng of golf fans being bottle-necked through an exit under some stands. Above us Europeans are drinking and singing 'Cheerio, cheerio, cheerio' to the droves of disgruntled Americans shuffling by. Nothing the Yanks can do except endure it – they're hemmed in – but they're not happy. The day has spread a patina of doubt over their identity as winners, as the best there is. Sport can do that. The certainties that they enjoyed (loudly) this morning before play have been scattered in the air like tightly clipped grass from a lawn mower. Now they are tetchy and anxious to be away from the scene of their humiliation; back to the comforting reality of their no-doubt palatial and well-secured North Chicago homes.

A tall, crew-cut man close by says: 'If it weren't for us in World War II, you'd all be talkin' German now,' and some Americans chuckle mirthlessly. The Europeans, including me and some nearby Germans, just smile and scuffle on. Our silent smiles are the loudest and clearest reminders of the impossible reality of what just happened.

My hands are on the shoulders of my ten-year-old son, Jack,

keeping him close. He is nervous, I can tell, with so many people pressing in all around. The mood of the Americans is as dark as the shadows of the surrounding tall trees, pulsing an air of male hostility that is pressing in on him. I lean down to him and whisper in his ear.

'Who won?' I say.

'We won,' Jack replies – our stock phrase. He looks up and I wink at him and smile and he smiles back and gives a shiver of excitement. You know the one, that suppressed glee that makes children shake or wiggle in an effort to hold it in. He can't wait to recount to his mother and sister all the wonders of the day when we get back to Mary and Chris's home in Winnetka. I squeeze his shoulders reassuringly and scratch his scalp. He loves that and he presses his head against my fingers.

Likewise, I can't wait to phone my mother and tell her all about the day. She'll have the phone by her chair near the fire waiting for my report. We'll talk about Seve Ballesteros whose memory lifted the twelve European players to make real a clarity of vision that nothing could undo today. Not the on-fire USA team, the hostile fans, nor the ridiculously easy placement of the pins. How she loved Seve, that irrepressible and beautiful free spirit of the game.

I can see her in that old room, the embers of the early autumn fire whispering in the grate. The photos of myself and my brothers and sisters and my nephews and nieces on the mantelpiece – the one of my wedding in prime place because Mam looked so well in it. Trophies and bric-a-brac on the dresser beside the lamp, her good china behind its glass doors.

I sigh and smile again. All's well. All's better than well in this reality.

I say 'this reality' because the picture I'm painting isn't strictly true. And the closer I come to the exit gate, the more it fades. It can't hold itself together much longer. There's a different reality breaking through from a different place and time.

One in which my mother died on 19 July 1997, of lung cancer, fifteen years before Medinah. In which my mother died on her seventy-sixth birthday and with maybe twenty years of good living ahead of her. When my brothers and sisters and I congregated around her bed telling her how much we loved her, before we said our last goodbyes.

So she won't get to see the Ryder Cup highlights tonight, or any other golf highlights, and I won't get to sit with her and chat about them. Or phone her and tell her all about it.

And she's not knitting a pretty sky-blue cardigan for my little girl, Roisín. Which brings me to another gloss-over this scene is struggling to maintain.

You see, I don't have a daughter Roisín, or a son Jack. My wife, Ciara, and I wanted children, but it never happened for us, not in this reality. Just as the longing of my family could not prevent my mother from leaving this world, Ciara's longing and my longing to share all our love with our children could not pull Roisín and Jack into it.

I see them, Jack at ten and Roisín at seven standing in a kind of doorway or waiting area, hand in hand. Jack has a solemn look on his face, the kind that small boys have. He's wearing a Cork jersey (of course he is) and white togs and yellow boots with the laces open. Roisín is in a summer dress and sandals. She's more of a Coghlan (Ciara's family), the image of her uncle Kevin at that age. She has a small scrape on her knee.

They're not distressed or sad, I can't bring myself to imagine that, they're just … there, and not here, not with us where they should be.

Except in moments like these, in that liminal space between two realities – under the light of these timeless heightened unreal sporting brilliances – when anything seems possible, is possible. When dreams and realities coalesce and different truths thread themselves through my mind, giving physical form and the momentary presence of that which will never be.

My wonderful secondary school English teacher, the late Ollie Ryan, told me a story. It was in 1999, a year after my father's death and two years after I'd lost my mother. Ollie was a kind man and I owe him a lot – I probably would not be a writer but for him.

The story was that, when Manchester United won the Champions League a few months earlier (in very dramatic circumstances), he picked up the phone to ring his father to share the amazing news. He dialled the number and then realised that his father had been dead for ten years. He put the phone back down.

He told me the story to prepare me for the waves of loss that would flow over me for the rest of my life.

I thought a lot about Ollie ringing his father ten years after his death. The incredible excitement of United's two goals at the end of a game that seemed a lost cause. A European Cup Final, bringing him back to 1968, perhaps, when he had at last watched United become champions of Europe, his father beside him. When Ollie was young and his father could enjoy such joys with him.

What was going on while Ollie dialled the number to talk to his father? What was he feeling, what was his reality?

In those moments – between the end of the match and the slap of actuality that hit him – Ollie Ryan's father *was* alive. The joy of Manchester United's famous win had – miraculously – brought his father back to life. His father was present and Ollie was about to share the most incredible news with him.

In his book *What We Think About When We Think About Football*, the philosopher Simon Critchley tells a similar story. He is in Goodison Park at the Merseyside derby – he's a big Liverpool fan. He is with his young son and his nephew, who is older. In the queue for food, he sees his father in a parallel queue up ahead. But his father is dead.

'I mean,' he writes, 'it was him. I felt sure it was him.' He stares at what he takes to be his father's ghost for the longest time, soaking in every feature. The same shape of face, the same gait, the same nose, the same olive, pock-marked skin, double chin and hair. It is his father for sure. But his father does not turn, nor acknowledge him.

Simon says nothing, brings the food to the boys and watches the match. Liverpool win 2–0 and Steven Gerrard scores. They are happy. In the car home, while his young son sleeps in the back, Simon sheepishly tells his nephew, Daniel, what he had seen. Daniel knew his father well, as a child.

Daniel says that he had seen him too.

Now, there are many plausible explanations for that occurrence. But the one that I believe is this: Simon Critchley's father *was* at that game with him. Football and his family and Liverpool

Football Club had drawn him there. Or, more accurately, Simon's love of football, his family and Liverpool Football Club had drawn his father there; back to his son and his grandsons.

In August 2018 Limerick won the All-Ireland Hurling Championship for the first time in almost half a century. The scenes of joy after the event were extraordinary; that so many had been so moved and affected by a sporting event. In response, I was moved to write this piece for the *Irish Examiner*:

Hurling is in the Quiet, not the Noise

I saw two photos on Sunday, on the magnificent, blissful day that Limerick attained Nirvana and won the All-Ireland Hurling Senior Championship for the first time in forty-five years.

The two photos summed up hurling for me. Sport, really, but hurling particularly.

The first was posted on Twitter by a Limerick man. It is of a cross on his father's grave. His father only died last February so there isn't a headstone yet, just one of those temporary wooden crosses we have to put up with for a year or so.

Around the top section of the cross, somebody had tied a green and white headband.

And the man had posted the photo on Twitter to thank whoever put it there.

I suspect he had gone to the grave on Saturday evening or Sunday morning before he travelled to Dublin to the game. Now why do you think he did that in the first place?

On that specific day? There's a lot on, a lot to do. Why go to the grave on that day?

Why do you think? You know why. I don't have to tell you.

And he saw the headband there. Wrapped lovingly there, by somebody – he didn't know whom.

Now, what did that mean to him? Can you imagine that moment, when he passed the other graves, along a familiar path? Said a quiet hello, maybe, to somebody leaving the graveyard?

Then he saw the little splash of green and white on the brown wooden cross. Perhaps he was with his daughter or his son, or his wife. Perhaps he was with his widowed mother. Can you imagine how he felt at that moment? Did he put his hand to his mouth? Were his eyes dry? Did he say something?

That's hurling. That single moment. Right there, distilled all the way down to the emotion when you see some unexpected green and white on a cross.

Family is everything, Micheál Donoghue said, tearfully, last year after he put the cup into his father Miko's hands in Ballinasloe the day after the final.

Family is everything. And hurling is family. So, what does that make hurling?

The second photo was posted on Twitter too by a writer I know from Kilkenny, on the day that was in it. The photo was of her father at a match. A close shot from the side, he's reading a programme I think, and he has a black and amber headband around his neck.

She must have lost her father recently, too, because

she posted of how she was thinking of him yesterday, of how often they'd gone to finals together to cheer on their beloved Kilkenny.

Of course she was. Of course she did.

And do you think that many graveyards were visited on Sunday evening and Monday morning in County Limerick?

I think they were.

Can you picture those scenes and what the people standing by the graves were thinking, remembering, saying? In the quiet of the graveyard?

How deep does hurling go?

How deep do you think it goes?

It's not in the shouting at final whistles that we see the real meaning of hurling, of sport. Not even in the headline shot on the front of sports sections of newspapers.

It's not in the screaming that deafened the gods, on Sunday in Croke Park. Or last night when that team entered that stadium on the Ennis Road. Yes, it's there too, don't get me wrong, when we see young women and men in ecstasy hug each other and old men and women weep amid the din.

This is the externalisation of sport, the flow out from within. And it's lovely, and we need it and love it.

But the place that hurling really dwells is deeper within. Buried there, for a long time. In the quiet. In the quiet of a photo above the television that you went to and touched when the final whistle blew on Sunday. The hat still hanging in the utility room because you can't bring yourself to move it, but glance at every day. The grave you promise yourself you'll look after better, now that there's a bit of rain and growth again.

Or when you suddenly see your late mother in your young son's eyes. And how your Mam loved to go to matches, how it made her feel so alive, so herself.

And your son suddenly says: are you okay, Mam? And you smile at him and give him a hug and do not speak, but remain quiet.

That's hurling.

Right there. In the quiet.

As I say, I wrote the article in response to the emotional outpouring after Limerick's stunning All-Ireland win against Galway. But I also wrote it in response to a story a friend told me, who saw something strange when she was visiting a family grave in St Otteran's Cemetery in Waterford City in June 2002.

She was just about to leave the cemetery when car after car began to pull up outside. Dozens of people moved past her, walking to graves – mostly men and they were mostly crying.

Waterford had just won the Munster hurling final – for the first time since 1963 – and the first thing that the men walking past her had done was to head straight to their family graves after the game. They did this to share the moment with loved ones whom they had lost. They did this to tell those people about the game – just as Ollie Ryan had phoned his father.

They did this because on that day in 2002 their loved ones had come back to them, and they needed to pass on some incredible news.

What is it about sport that made the Galway hurling captain, David Burke, leave two sliotars on the grave of his former team-mate Niall Donoghue on the night before the All-Ireland hurling final of 2017? Why, immediately after the 2020 All-Ireland hurling final, did the Limerick captain Declan Hannon speak about three people who had passed away the previous week? Why does Nickie Quaid keep his father's memorial card in his gear bag and visit his grave before every championship game? What is it about sport that makes the Mullinalaghta St Columba's Gaelic football team call into the local graveyard before celebrating every championship they win?

It may be that we, the living, want to remember those who have gone before us and to respect the sacrifices they made. Or it may be that we, the living, want to share great moments with those whom we have lost; and in that sharing, those whom we have lost are regained.

And these are the miracles of sport.

KISSES

I HAVE ONLY ONE MEMORY OF MY father kissing me. I was eighteen years old. It happened on the long curved platform of Kent Station, Cork, the night after the All-Ireland hurling final of 1979, when my teammates and I brought the Minor cup home.

I can recall almost nothing about the match, but I clearly remember the railway station being packed with giddy people when the train eked itself out of the tunnel and braked to a stop. A pipe and drum band was playing full blast. From the door of the train I saw my father approaching through the crowd. I felt the pull of his arms as I stepped down on the platform. I saw the liquid joy in his eyes. The startling bristle of his stubble on my cheek and the scent of whiskey from his breath are as vivid to me today as if it all happened yesterday.

His voice is hoarse with passion. 'Oh, Tadhg, oh, Tadhg. I'm so proud of you. I'm so proud.'

I'm sure my father kissed me as a child; he was a loving and tactile man. I remember his bedtime stories about last-minute rescues in helicopters, but I can't remember any of those kisses. I'm sure he was proud of me on the day I graduated (eventually) from university, and on the day I got married, and the times I looked after him and my mother when they were elderly.

But I let him down in so many ways. I never won a county with Mallow. I flunked out of college and caused him years of worry. I was never successful, financially. I never gave him a grandchild. Despite these failings he was endlessly loyal to me.

In August 1998 my father was living in a nursing home. He was eighty and had become very frail since my mother had died the previous summer. Ciara and I were on our way to a wedding in Galway and, as we approached Mallow, she asked if I wanted to call in to see him. I said no, we'd keep going, and he died the following night while I was drinking and dancing at the wedding.

It isn't surprising that I watch out for photos or videos of such kisses in the sports pages of newspapers after games.

In the epic semi-final of the All-Ireland Senior Hurling Championship, in August 2017, Galway beat Tipperary by a single point in Croke Park. Joe Canning was the hero of the Tribesmen, with a score in the dying moments of the game like some otherworldly feat by a Homeric demi-god. All his life beforehand had led him up to that moment. All his life afterwards is leading away from it.

There is a picture of Joe being embraced by his mother, Josephine, after the game. The camera is on her, from behind and to the left of Joe. She looks at him; her eyes, uplifted, are radiating love and pride, her smile is motherly and tender. Her hands are raised, her fingers are touching his chest – she has already hugged him or is about to. His eyes appear closed or downcast. Perhaps he is tearful too, we don't know. He looks spent. Reposeful. He carries his warrior helmet in his left hand. Sweat glistens from the short hairs on his head and at the nape of his neck.

Something is passing between them. Why he does this, how he can do this. For whom he is really doing all this. For whom all sportspeople are really doing this.

Another image is from Ballinasloe on the day after Galway won the All-Ireland a few weeks after Joe Canning's heroics. They bring the Liam McCarthy Cup home and cross the border at Ballinasloe. Here the bus pulls up and Micheál Donoghue, the team manager, puts the cup into the hands of his elderly father, Miko, who is sitting in a wheelchair with a rug over his lap by the side of the road. A photo of the moment shows the cup in the foreground; it shines. The Celtic engraving entwined around the silvery metal is prominent. Miko is weeping.

Miko is weeping with joy and pride and because he thought he'd never see the cup come west of the Shannon again before he died. And to think, to think that his own son, his very own Micheál made that happen. Micheál's eyes are downcast and his lips are set to prevent him from crying, too. He has put a consoling arm around his father and their foreheads are pressed together in a sweet and timeless intimacy.

Another image of a father and son struck me in March 2018. The Australian cricket captain, Steve Smith, was found to have cheated in a test match against South Africa by tampering with the ball. His career was in ruins, he had lost huge amounts of money as a professional and he was utterly disgraced. Australia is not a forgiving place when it comes to sporting failure. This was a long and bruising fall; there were many striking him on the way down, including the British tabloids who nicknamed him 'Captain Cry Baby'.

On arrival back to Sydney, he tearfully apologised, but it wasn't until he mentioned the impact on his father and mother that he completely broke down. It wasn't the money, or his reputation, or the worldwide shame he had brought to Australian cricket that distressed him so much as the devastation of his father, who was standing beside him, trying to help him through the press conference.

We regularly see moments of intimacy such as hugs and kisses at sporting events. At golf events, husbands, wives and children greet victors on 18th greens under the frenzied gaze of the media. Children rush out onto the grass to be joyfully lifted up by their champion mothers and fathers at the moment of glory. Fans cheer and smile and clap their hands in a ritualistic homage as old as time. The trophy and the glory are not the only prizes for the successful, these images boast. A beautiful wife or a handsome husband, or happy, healthy, wealthy children are included in the spoils of professional sport.

But what about the losers? What about the golfers who have blown the four-shot lead, to come up short? What about the goalkeepers who have conceded soft goals, the strikers who have missed crucial penalties? The rugby players who have been sent off after moments of madness, disgracing themselves?

Their hugs and kisses are of a different intimacy: consolatory, bestowed in quiet corners, as fans and media lower their heads and look away, offering a respectful and sympathetic privacy.

In June 2018, after Tipperary's final round-robin match in

the Munster Hurling Championship, I watched my television as ecstatic Clare fans invaded the pitch after a dramatic win. Tipperary were out, beaten on their own patch, in the most agonising of circumstances.

As the Clare players jumped around and hugged each other and were swamped by adoring fans, I caught a glimpse of a Tipperary player on his knees, crying inconsolably. I won't say his name. I could see a middle-aged woman trying to console him. The camera moved on and I did not rewind to have a closer look, although I wanted one. It wouldn't have been right.

I was amazed at how quickly the woman had reached the player and I wondered if she was his mother, or another concerned Tipperary woman, or even some Clare fan who could see his distress and tried to console him in the moment. I'll never know.

Parental love and kisses are one thing, romantic love and kisses are another.

The FIFA Women's World Cup in the summer of 2019 was a wonderful and significant occasion on many levels. At last, the great women footballers of the world got the attendances at games, the viewership, and the media attention they deserved. There were other significant elements to the championship I'll go into later, to do with sexism and homophobia.

The best team in the world, the USA, deservedly won the cup and, after the final, several of the players ran to the fans' zone reserved for family and friends, to celebrate.

The fans are in a raised stand above the pitch and the players have to step up on the backs of chairs and stretch to get close to their loved ones. One of the players, Kelley O'Hara, a native of

Georgia, has to lean forward awkwardly to kiss her girlfriend – in effect, O'Hara was coming out by this kiss, she hadn't previously declared herself as gay, unlike forty-one of the other players involved in the tournament.

To prolong the moment she pulls herself up by a metal bar and holds herself suspended a few feet over the ground. The photo that drew me in most was the one taken just after the kiss. Our view is from the side and behind and we cannot see O'Hara's eyes. Her upturned head looks almost supplicating, desperate for approbation.

Her hair is long and ponytailed, and slick with sweat at the side. The faces of the two women are touching. O'Hara's girlfriend is above her and she has cupped the footballer's neck with her left hand; a thumb around the ear. She has gold rings around her middle and wedding fingers. A pendant is hanging from her neck, mid-air. Her eyes are almost closed, with what looks like the remnants of a tear below the left one. Her lips are slightly parted, in the beginning of a smile.

It is a perfect moment of shared intimacy, joy and love, granted to these two people by sport.

'Family is everything,' Micheál Donoghue said in an interview, trying to maintain his composure, when the cup came home to Ballinasloe on that September day, in 2017. What he didn't say, but what was said in the image of him and Miko (and in the other images) is that sport and love and family are as bound together and intertwined as the Celtic engraving on the Liam McCarthy Cup. Micheál became the coach of the Galway hurling team so that he could have such a moment of intimacy with his father.

I write about sport because of my father's kiss in 1979. And because of all the other kisses, by all the other fathers and mothers and brothers and sisters and friends and wives and girlfriends and husbands and boyfriends and coaches and teammates and delirious fans.

But my father's kiss is not only the reason I write about sport – it's the reason I write at all. I am writing to find a way to pass on my father's kiss.

I wrote about such a kiss and built a story around it ('Dúchas') and built a book (*The First Sunday in September*) around that story. Because I can never have that kiss again, I was compelled to write one. I wanted to give thanks for it and to mourn it. My book was published on the twentieth anniversary of my father's death and I allowed myself to confer some significance in that.

I wrote a story where a man kisses his son, who has captained his county to an All-Ireland championship. The kiss is witnessed by the hurler's birth father, who gave him up for adoption as a baby and realises that he will never bestow such a kiss to his son. I know this sense of loss. I don't have a daughter or a son and so I will never pass on my father's kiss. In reality, that kiss dies with me. My writing of it is an attempt to pass it on. A pale shadow of the real thing, but in that writing I don't feel so alone, or so lost without my father and my children.

We read stories and I write stories because they go beyond fact into a deeper truth, the kind that Julian Barnes was referring to when he said that literature is 'the best way of telling the truth … a process of producing grand, beautiful, well-ordered lies that tell more truth than any assemblage of facts'.

And so I can rewrite the facts that my mother and father are dead and Jack and Roisín were never born. I can transform them into a different reality, a different truth – one in which my mother and father are with Jack and Roisín in the living room of our house on the Cork Road, Mallow. They are watching golf together on the television and Roisín – I see her sitting on my mother's lap – is asking question after question because she doesn't understand the game. She's tired and cranky but she'd face a regiment, the same one, and won't give in to it.

My father smiles and my mother gently explains the game to Roisín while Jack glances at the photos on the mantelpiece. One photo is of me on my wedding day beside my best man – my brother Padraig – and my mother and father. I'm smiling broadly – it is the happiest day of my life. My father's old blade putter with the worn green handle is by Jack's side as it usually is; he practises with it obsessively in the long carpeted hall.

What if my writing creates another layer of this alternative reality and confers its munificence to me?

What if the door opens and Ciara and I walk in and our beautiful children run to us and we kiss them? Passing on all the kisses we received from our mothers and fathers; passing on all the kisses handed down forever, through time, with love.

PART 3

INITIATIONS, LONGING

TO BELONG

I don't really like being so emotional about Sunderland, but I am. And of course it has nothing to do with whichever bunch of players happens to be wearing the candystripes this season. Nothing to do with the manager, the style of play or success. It's to do with home, and family, and a sense of the club as representative of a strand of belonging stretching back generations.

– Jonathan Wilson

I T IS 1971 AND I AM ten years old. I am watching the Cork hurler Con Roche take a sideline cut on a hot day in a heaving Semple Stadium, in Thurles. Thirty-two thousand other people are present in this moment around me. I am with my father and some of the Walsh family – old friends – and my older brother Dermot has just played with the Cork Minors, winning the Munster hurling final.

We are beside the sideline and I have a good view of Roche as he bends down and places the sliotar on the grass. He stands back and lowers his torso in his approach to the ball, as hurlers do. The hurley is swung hard, at an acute angle, into the sliotar. We are so close that I can hear the sound of the hurley's heel slashing into the earth – a dull, meaty thud. The other sound of the hurley's *bas* striking the ball: a gravid 'pock'. The ball rising towards the Tipperary goal, the pitch of the crowd's anticipation rising too – it's a great cut. The ball falling towards the goal, the sound of the crowd deepening and mounting, expectant.

There's a slight shimmer in the distant net and a different noise detonates itself. A concussive wave booms and rolls through the stadium as though it is a living thing, bellowing its approval.

I sometimes wonder if I'm seeking the sound of that crowd at every game I attend. If it is the cause of my desperate exultation as I sit in the stand and the match approaches. I'm like an addict craving that first high I experienced when I was ten.

My eyes wide in circles of wonder. My mouth open in a silent *oh*.

Experiencing that sideline cut compels me, as a boy, to incessantly hone skills and devote myself to playing. Which, in turn, leads to my presence on that same pitch in Thurles, only six years later, playing for St Colman's College, Fermoy, in an All-Ireland colleges final against St Kieran's College, Kilkenny. Johnny Lenihan, the captain and one of the leading players in the team, has been injured, and I am drafted in at wing back to replace him.

I am only sixteen years old and it is my first Senior colleges game. It is also my first All-Ireland final and I have only three memories of the match.

Trying not to show my discomfort when my marker approaches me before the game. He is six inches taller than me, and six inches wider. He has a beard and looks about twenty-five.

Waving frantically to the sideline in the first half when our centre back and lynchpin, Seanie O'Brien, is knocked out beside me and I'm thinking, *That's it, we're beat now.*

Winning possession near the final whistle, I have a sense of having the ball on the ground before me. I am running and guiding it past an opponent to a teammate – hockey-style – and it leads to a goal by Jimmy Monaghan. I have no idea how.

Years later my brother-in-law Michael Harrington – a real hurling man – told me I flicked the ball away from a St Kieran's player as he was about to strike, then caught it and cleared it up the field for John Boylan to win possession and create the goal for Jimmy, but I can't visualise it. According to *The Irish Times* the following day I was 'an outstanding figure in defence' but I can't visualise that, either. I have no memory of it, in any case.

I have no recollection of the final whistle, being mobbed by schoolmates and friends. I have no memory of my family being there, the cup presentation, the speeches, the dressing room afterwards, the journey back or the celebrations – nothing. All of that must have happened and I must have been part of it. It must have been amazing to a quiet and innocent sixteen-year-old boy. But it's all a blank.

Hours after the game I bump into our coach, the charismatic John Whyte, who had gambled heavily (against strong opposition from within the school) by putting me in at wing back. It is outside the Grand Hotel by the river in Fermoy. He grabs me by the shoulders and grins. He smells of smoke and drink and tells me I was the man of the match.

After that day, after that game, I was a hurler – I was a serious player – I know this now.

Being a player doesn't mean skill, so much as being able to use that skill and do a job for your team in serious circumstances, when something serious is happening and you are playing against serious players, for serious stakes. An All-Ireland final qualifies as serious stakes, even at secondary-school level. There were thousands of people at the game and it was in Semple Stadium. And the opposition was Kilkenny.

You often hear the expression 'He's a born hurler,' or 'She's a born footballer.' In truth, nobody is born a player, you become one.

At some time in my childhood a switch was flicked inside me, giving light to an idea. Giving life to the presence – the lifelong presence – of sport in my consciousness. Was it that Con Roche moment in Thurles in 1971? Perhaps. It was probably more than one event and my brother Dermot winning an All-Ireland Minor medal with Cork that year was more than likely a major spark. Or the sense of wonder in my father's eyes, the reverence in his voice, when he talked about hurlers like Christy Ring and Mick Mackey. Or watching Dermot and other Mallow heroes win a county championship in 1972. Or the sight of George Best's immeasurable beauty when he scored again and again and again in 1968; his impossible grace; his promise making all promises possible, all futures pliant and fine, all bodily movement a kind of magnificent, inevitable, riparian flow.

I don't think my initiation to sport was any different to many others. I have asked several people interested in sport (players, ex-players, sportswriters and fans) how they were initiated and it's often the childhood memory of their father bringing them to a game, or how much it meant that their father watched them play.

In his memoir, *Recovering*, Richie Sadlier writes about his lack of self-confidence as a child, how he feared calamity around every corner. And how his longing for his father's approval and his desire that his father would watch him play drove him on to excel at football. When, aged eleven, he was asked at a group therapy session with his father (who was being treated for alcoholism at the time) what one thing would he ask of his father, he said: 'I just want him to watch me play football.'

This desire led Sadlier to become a professional footballer in England and an Irish international.

Such initiations are not confined to sport.

The singer songwriter Annie Erin Clark (St. Vincent) said that at the very moment she heard Nirvana's album *Nevermind* – when she was twelve – she knew how she would spend her life.

She had always felt like an outsider – a 'weirdo' – as a child. But *Nevermind* affirmed that status and, at the same time, made it acceptable. She knew, from Kurt Cobain and Nirvana, where she belonged and if she belonged outside her Texas upbringing's values and societal norms, so be it. She knew, even as a child, where she wanted to be. And she knew she would find a way to get there.

Richie Sadlier, and so many other sportspeople (including me), felt at home on a pitch; we belonged there. Annie Clark felt at home on a stage with a guitar.

It felt *right*, and so it was right.

We had been initiated. We belonged.

Belonging, being part of something (something bigger) – feeling at home somewhere – brings a sense of rightness and possibility. Belonging is no longer being alienated, no longer being different, no longer being alone, no longer being outside looking in. Belonging is being inside, belonging is being one of many, belonging is longing answered, belonging is no longer being lost. Belonging is being found.

In *Belonging: Remembering Ourselves Home,* the Canadian writer, teacher and dreamworker Toko-pa Turner points out different types of belonging:

> The first kind that comes to mind is the feeling of belonging in a community, or to a geography. But for many of us, longing to belong begins in our own families. Then there is the longing we feel to belong with an intimate other in the sanctuary of relationship, and the belonging we yearn to feel in a purpose or vocation. There is also spiritual longing to belong to a set of ways or traditions, the longing to know and participate in ancestral knowledge. And, though we may not even notice how its severance influences us, the ache to belong in our own bodies.

Sport satisfies so many of these yearnings to belong. Through sport we can belong to communities, places, families, relationships, vocations, ancestral knowledge, traditions, our own bodies, the creation of our own stories and to something greater than ourselves which gives our lives meaning.

John McGahern writes in his book *Memoir* about spending time as a child with a local man, Eddie McIniff, with whom he used to pick potatoes. He uses his name (but not his character) in the short story 'Eddie Mac'.

Eddie, who played on the Ballinamore Gaelic football team, gave McGahern lessons in how to take frees by practising kicking potatoes over a ditch – until they were caught by McGahern's father. When Ballinamore beat McGahern's local team Aghawillan the young McGahern waited afterwards to congratulate Eddie, who had starred in the game. Eddie lifted him in the air and said 'Shawneen boy!' and McGahern, who was delighted, said, in tears, 'You played great, Eddie,' and he felt proud and absolved and happy.

McGahern – who let sport into his life (perhaps after moments like that one at a Leitrim final, or after Ulster finals he went to with his father) and is one of the few Irish writers to use sport in his fiction – knew the power of sport to conquer the child's heart and the man's heart. In his short story 'Love of the World', Guard Harkin is a famous footballer, playing midfield for Mayo and a potential All-Star. Kate Ruttledge falls in love with him and, though she had shown no interest in any sport until then, spends a rainy summer travelling to matches all around the county. She witnesses 'men and boys look long and deep into his face, lost in the circle and dream of his fame'. She holds her breath as he rides 'the shoulders of running mobs bearing him in triumph from pitches'.

I'm sure, as a child, that I looked long and deep into the faces of great local Mallow hurlers like Tommy Sheehan, Liam Sheehan, Pat Healy, Paddy Buckley and Paddy Carey. I'm sure, as a child, that I would have run onto pitches when Mallow won games and at any acknowledgement from such men felt proud and happy, absolved, lost in the circle and dream of their fame. And the fact that my brother Dermot was one of those heroes would have given me inordinate pride and perhaps sowed the seed that I, someday, could play hurling for my club and be the hero, too.

In the summer of 1979, the year when I was a Cork Minor hurler, I was working in the cattle mart in Mallow.

I remember going into the toilet in the mart – which is not to be mistaken with the gents' toilet in the Ritz Carlton on the Place Vendôme, in Paris. I was wearing my brown drover's coat and wellington boots over old overalls.

Having taken my pee and washed my hands, I heard a man with a young boy say: 'See him? He's a Cork Minor.' I turned and smiled at the boy.

He looked up at me as I retrieved my stick, with the sounds of cattle bellowing in the distance and an auctioneer's amplified voice droning from the sales ring nearby.

I can still see his little round face, shining in the way that only children's faces can shine. His eyes are wide in circles of wonder. His mouth is open in a silent *oh*.

MEMORIES –

PECULIAR VERACITIES

IN 2020, WHILE RESEARCHING ANOTHER BOOK, I made some startling discoveries about the match in which Con Roche scored a goal from a sideline cut when I was ten years old. The moment that evoked the crowd's exultation and a great sense of wonder in me. My initiation into sport which I remember so vividly.

I discovered that Con Roche did not score a goal that day, let alone direct from a sideline cut. The goal never happened; in fact he scored a point from the sideline cut. Secondly, Cork weren't playing Tipperary, but Limerick. Thirdly, Cork lost that day, despite my memory of us winning. And my brother Dermot didn't win a Minor medal that day, either – it was a day of semi-finals, not finals.

My memory has tricked me, as memories do. Something

in me wanted that memory to be true and so I made it true. In the way that family members remember a Christmas spat or a drunken-uncle drama differently – each bringing their own brush to the white canvas of the event (what they want to remember) and filling it in accordingly.

The stories/memories that we take out of the sporting moments of our childhoods, or our own sporting experiences (or lack thereof), may not be based on facts or what actually happened, but they are real and they are true, nonetheless.

In a way, by writing down the story of Con Roche's goal, I made it true. By expressing it in words, I imprinted it on my memory as being a real memory. This is called verbal overshadowing – a term coined by Jonathan W. Schooler and Tonya Engstler-Schooler. The act of writing the event (a dramatic and vivid moment in a game, witnessed by a child) in the way I wrote it, overshadows – or takes precedent over – the actual event and becomes my memory of what actually happened. My saying it was true makes it true. The real remembering is in the telling.

As a writer, this concept and this occurrence give me great joy.

It doesn't matter if my recollections of a game in 1971 are accurate or strictly true. They are true in a greater sense, a more marvellous sense, with their own particular veracities.

Brian Friel explored memory and truth in *Philadelphia, Here I Come!*. In the play he recreated a scene from his own childhood, where a nine-year-old boy and his father are walking down a muddy path by a lake after a day's fishing. Although they are wet from rain, the boy's father is happy – they have caught several fish – and as they approach the village they begin to sing.

The only problem is that it never happened to him. Friel said in an interview: 'There is no lake along that muddy road. And since there is no lake, my father and I never walked back from it in the rain with our rods across our shoulders. The fact is a fiction.'

However, Friel insists: 'For me it is a truth. And because I acknowledge its peculiar veracity it becomes a layer in my subsoil; it becomes part of me; ultimately it becomes me.' This, too, is how I feel about Con Roche's sideline cut and the sound of the crowd that day in 1971. They have become part of me; they have become a layer in my subsoil; they have forged something inside me.

In his memoir *Over the Backyard Wall*, Thomas Kilroy (who captained the St Kieran's College Senior hurling team in 1952) says that fiction is another avenue of retrieval, one that is intimately related to memory. 'It is, in fact,' he says, 'an imaginative imitation of the process of memory.' What happened and what is remembered meld together like two rivers meeting and after the melding they are one river, as though they were always one river.

Fintan O'Toole, in a 2015 *Irish Times* article about Friel, says: 'In *Philadelphia*, that first great play ... the very power with which [the illusory memory] is evoked on stage lifts it into a different kind of reality. It makes its own truth. That trajectory, from reality to fiction to shattered illusion and back to a sort of heightened presence, is the journey of a Friel play.'

Sport's heightened presence is also part of my life's journey and it feeds this book and all my writing.

Sport feeds my memories and it makes its own truth.

Richie Sadlier also has such false memories. He remembers, as a boy, going to St Patrick's Athletic games with his father in Harold's Cross, their temporary home.

In his memory, he writes, his father brought him many times. But his friend, who was there every week, told him years later that his father very rarely went to those games.

Sadlier's longing to go to games with his father turned that longing into a memory.

A Cork sportswriter, Michael Russell, told me a similar story. One of his earliest sporting memories was of going to a football game in Kilcohan Park, between Waterford and Cork Celtic. It was in 1963 and he was ten years old. His father dropped him at the grounds and picked him up after the game.

When he told this to his older brother years later, his brother laughed and said it never happened. He said: 'Do you really think Dad would drop his ten-year-old son to a game like that and leave him there on his own?'

A cousin of Michael's recently told him that far from being alone at that game, his father, his uncle, his brother and two cousins were with him. But in his memory of the game, Michael was alone. It never happened, but he clearly remembers it.

I'm always amazed at how little memory I have of my playing days.

I played football for the Mallow United first team for six or seven years. I can visualise the Town Park in Mallow and a few other grounds. Sometimes I'll be driving around Cork and I might go past a pitch (say the Ringmahon Rangers pitch in Mahon). And if I get out and stand at the side of the grounds I will be able to scratch the surface of a memory of playing there – something vague, some inconsequential moment in a game, something another player said to me, or a score. I don't know if those memories are true or not, but they do seem real.

For a few years with Mallow United I played as a striker and I do remember scoring the odd goal. One, a header against St Mary's, was remarkable because I'm only five foot seven and it was from a corner kick, but somehow I got my head to the ball and it looped over the keeper and into the goal.

I remember scoring a goal when we played down the road from our house in the Back Field and I got a great pass from Daniel O'Callaghan and hit it first time with my right foot into the far corner. Maybe I remember that because I'm left-footed or because Aidan Warner (my brother-in-law) was there and I was proud when he saw me score. Now I wonder if those goals happened, or if I imagined them or idealised them as I seem to have done for the Con Roche sideline cut.

I've been told that I scored thirty goals one year when we won a league, but I have no memory of any of them or of winning the league.

I'm surprised when I meet people and they can tell me about games I played in and what I did. Goals I scored or blocks I made or people I marked, or whatever. I played hurling for twenty years for my club, Mallow, and I have only a handful of memories of that. Some of those games happened over forty years ago, so I'm not surprised I don't remember them in detail, but surely there should be more.

Some memories I do wish for.

I wish I could remember some of the faces on the train station at Mallow in 1979 when a great crowd came to greet my team and myself (as the only Mallow player) with the Minor All-Ireland cup that we had won for Cork. I wish I could remember meeting my mother and my brothers and sisters in the station – they must have been there, Padraig and Pauline especially. I do wish I could remember my mother's face that day.

I gave my hurleys to a club stalwart, Wally Hammond, to mind them for some reason – I have no idea why. I said some words, having been coached on public speaking on the train for ten seconds by the late great Christy Coughlan, our captain. Christy told me to say three things: to thank everybody for coming; to thank my own club, Mallow, for their support; and 'Up the Rebels!'

I have no idea if I followed his advice. I wish I could remember what I said and what it felt like on the platform. I wish I could remember the looks on people's faces, girls especially, that evening. It must have been something, but it's not there.

An hour later, in Cork city, I have my father's kiss.

At least I can remember that.

Between championship and challenge games in hurling and football, I must have played hundreds of matches for my hometown and attended a thousand training sessions, but I only have a vague sense of it all. It's like it happened to another person, who told me about it once, in a bar.

I remember losing three county finals, but those losses are encompassed within a sense of dread in that moment when you realise that the game is ebbing away and it's too late to rescue it. The inescapable truth of a bitter knowledge is looming over you. The sportswriter Simon Barnes puts it like this: the dark experiences of failure tell you without compromise, that 'you are less of a person than you hoped'. But I can't recall individual moments, acts or scenes from those losing finals, what the memory researcher Julie Shaw calls 'episodic memories'.

I was at a memorial to the great coach Canon Michael O'Brien in 2013 in UCC and one of my old teammates from the 1980s, Rory Duane from Tipperary, said: 'Ah, Jesus, Tadhg, you were something, lad.'

I was shocked. I don't remember being something. I did play on the team for four years and I captained it one year, but I remember so little of it. Tiny snippets. I wish I could remember more. Being something sounds good, I hope I felt like something, too, those days, but I doubt it.

In a way, by not remembering being a player – perhaps a serious player, perhaps something – I am creating another false memory of myself. Maybe some part of me doesn't want to remember any great things I did in sport, any achievements that I can hang my hat on. Because, if I did remember them, then they would be true and I'd be forced to unpick how I feel about myself.

In 2019 I was in Charleville for a newspaper article I was writing for the *Irish Examiner*, and I met an old buddy of mine, with whom I used to play football. We began chatting about old times; he was selling flags the same day.

'Do you still have the record?' he asked me.

'What record?' I said.

'The record for goals for a Cork Minor in one year,' he said, looking at me oddly.

I shook my head.

'Didn't you score five goals in three matches for the Cork Minors in '79?' he said.

'I did, yeah,' I replied. And I had done that. I knew I had done that but I'd forgotten it. Imagine forgetting something like that.

Simon Barnes says that it's the moments of greatness that remain the most vivid in the memory – which is what sport is all about – but I can't agree. Those glimpses, he says, (however brief or illusory) of the 'endless vistas of eternity'. I can't see those views of eternity in anything I've done.

Perhaps I cannot remember individual scenes – scoring goals or winning championships, glorious final whistles – because I was too deep in the moment of those games to look out of them. Others, on the sideline, were somewhat removed from the intensity of the moment – in ordinary time – and so they can recall the scenes more clearly.

The philosopher Steven Connor points out that the Ancient Greeks classified time as either being *chronos* or *kairos*. *Chronos* is normal (ordinary) time, sequential, which Connor refers to as being an empty and meaningless succession of events. *Kairos*, however, is when this is transformed into something meaningful, into a moment of special inspiration or revelation. *Kairos* is, in fact, the suspension of time, or a moment out of time, and sport gives us that, as I showed in my essay 'Ekstasis'.

I sometimes wonder if I cannot remember most of my sporting life because I was too deep inside *kairos*. And when (after the game), I returned to *chronos*, I left my memories behind me. Like in a fairy story where a character travels to another world and cannot remember her adventures when she returns.

I have a sense of some big games, of nerves or winning or losing – big crowds, big stakes and some big stadiums – but very little detail. I have the same sense when experiencing a vivid concert or a moving art exhibition. I cannot recall many moments in those, either, just the sense that something immense is happening, that I'm feeling powerful emotions. A sense of significance. A sense of what Joyce Carol Oates (after Aristotle) felt about boxing, that something 'serious, complete and of a certain magnitude' was taking place before her. She also said that boxing subsumes its boxers as any ceremony subsumes its participants. Perhaps I was subsumed into the games I played, somehow, and I was and still am too far inside them to be able to see out or to exit them and see back in.

When Pete Sampras was asked what was going through his mind when he served an ace to save a Wimbledon final match against Andre Agassi, he replied, 'Absolutely nothing.' I have spoken to several sportspeople about what they were thinking about during games and they almost all told me that they can't remember what they were thinking about at any given time. They were focusing on the process, or the action at that moment – the job at hand. They were acting with instinct, with muscle memory.

In many cases, they are like me: they just can't remember. In many cases, just like me, they remember the losses more than the wins.

I was rooting around the attic a while back, looking for an old photo album, and I knocked over a stacked container. It contained old diaries and notes and my small box of sports medals. The box didn't have a top on it and some of the medals fell out. I found two empty red boxes (the medals always seemed to come wrapped in cotton wool in little red boxes), from which the medals must have fallen onto the cluttered floor of the attic. I noticed that neither of them was my Fitzgibbon Cup captain's medal from 1983 (which is different from the others and it has a little sticker outside with the word 'Capt') and I was glad. But the medals are still there on the floor of the attic somewhere. When I have time I'll tidy the place up and I'll probably find them. One of them may be my All-Ireland Minor medal – the one my father kissed me for winning.

According to Julie Shaw, accessing episodic memories can be like reliving multisensory experiences where we 'feel our toes in the sand, the sun against our skin, the breeze in our hair. We can picture the venue, the music, the people. These are the memories we cherish.' What I remember most in sport is losing and failing, not being good enough. Nothing to cherish at all.

I must have felt joy and completeness in some moments of those games, but I no longer have a sense of those emotions.

Thomas Kilroy says that there is a hazy romanticism in his recollection of his play as a child. The fair green behind his childhood home is a 'green place of games and play and the release of the imagination'. He knows he has romanticised those recollections, but he's okay with that.

We need this romanticised selective memory when it comes to sport. We need to purge our minds of rainy days, bad pints, bad sandwiches, bad losses and the interminable traffic on the way home after losing. Otherwise, what on earth would bring us out the next day? And the next day after that?

On that day in 1971 in Thurles, my imagination (like Kilroy's) had been released – the miracle that is sport was something too stunningly wonderful not to be imagined, nor that I might have a place in it. A place that I still have, five decades later.

Loss, as I will prove later, is endemic to sport. We know before any given game that we could lose. It might be very likely, a racing certainty, as the cliché goes. But we still turn up.

Our selective memories, with their peculiar veracities and marvellous truths (the good days, the great feats, the sunshine, the good pints and good sandwiches, the laughter, the camaraderie, the wins, the affirmations, the joys) carry us to the game – these are what bring us back and so we cling to them, each and every time when we approach the game. When we ready ourselves for wonder and for glory.

Do you remember where you were when you heard about 9/11? Of course you do. Why do you remember in detail where you were and what you were doing on 11 September 2001? Is it the momentum of the news, or is it the emotional impact of what had happened, what was happening to the Twin Towers at that moment? I believe that the emotion you felt that day burned its details into your consciousness forever.

This happens all the time in sport.

I vividly remember being in Crowley's Bar, in Bridge Street, Cork, with Padraig and Gerry McGarry and Joe Keegan when Manchester United won the Champions League final on 26 May 1999. I remember being in the Nally Stand of Croke Park at the All-Ireland hurling final of 1977. I remember being in the Killinan End terrace in Semple Stadium for the Munster hurling final in 1990 with Scally and Tom Crowley when Cork came on to the pitch and the clouds parted and the sun shone down upon them.

The list goes on and on. I remember so many games I watched, but so few I played in. I don't know why that is.

The American writer Siri Hustvedt says that emotion plays a vital role in memory. 'Indifference is the swiftest road to amnesia,' she says. I am not indifferent at big sporting moments.

And very few people were indifferent on 11 September 2001.

I'm not really distressed by my lack of memory of moments playing sport – even the good ones, of which, luckily, there were many. I had them, I lived them. I know them to be true. I can still remember some of the best ones, like my father's kiss, the joy and relief of captaining a winning Fitzgibbon Cup team, the sense of togetherness, shared purpose and friendship – love, perhaps – within teams. I am still remembered in Mallow for games I played and by some of the older players from UCC.

I also remember that game and that goal by Con Roche from 1971 – even if it never happened. I well remember my own little game, kicking my childhood football around my home on the Cork Road.

I'm sure that the activity of writing this book reformed some more memories of when I played sport and I will pay more attention from now on. Writing this will help me to study the new memories I acquire as a fan. I will gather them and write them down to hold on to them.

Ian Maleney, in his beautiful memoir *Minor Monuments*, writes about memory and his grandfather's wanderings within the memory desert that is Alzheimer's. He epigraphs one chapter with a quote from W.G. Sebald: 'The older you get, in a sense, the more you forget. Vast tracts of your life sort of vanish into oblivion. But that which survives in your mind acquires a very considerable degree of density, a very high degree of specific weight.' My memories of playing sport have this high specific weight, and writing them down has rendered them even denser. However much longer they are with me, I hold them dear.

In 2019 the sportswriter and historian Dave Hannigan wrote in *The Irish Times* about something called 'sports reminiscence therapy', whereby patients suffering from Alzheimer's and dementia in the United States are re-engaged with sports they loved and had lived with. By exposing the sights, sounds and paraphernalia of baseball, therapists are re-evoking and bringing back to life 'childhoods where fathers played catch with sons of an evening on the front lawns of the first iteration of suburban America'.

Doctors, Hannigan writes, 'believe this form of therapy taps into something called "the reminiscence bump", the part of the brain which allows us to remember most of the stuff that left a deep impression on us between the ages of 10 and 30 years old.' Family members sit in on the sessions for a treasured glimpse of a 'loved one's eyes lighting up afresh, revitalised by jumpy footage of a World Series or a sepia-tinted photograph of a pitcher they idolised as kids … Patients who barely speak start talking, sometimes in granular detail, about games they witnessed or

Little League encounters they played in when all their world was young.' And in that talking they are young again and are returned to their loved ones and families.

I imagine myself as an old man with dementia in years to come, sitting empty and inexpressive in such a nursing home. I imagine Ciara or a brother or sister – maybe a kind nephew or niece – bringing me one of my little red boxes containing a medal; those medals so neglected in my attic, two of them somewhere strewn on the ground up there. I imagine my old stubby fingers rubbing against the medal's ridges and the engraving of the symbols of the four provinces of Ireland. The four piercings in the middle. The little loop of metal at the top. The stylised Irish writing etched on the back. The colour: a deep and burnished gold.

I imagine memories coming back to me then. Memories of me, in a red jersey, with a hurley in my hands, being something, being somebody, again.

THE COLLECTIVE

Playing football in Cavan was what they call in our
business 'taking refuge in the collective'. Everybody
loves you, you're with the crowd, you're on the populated side of the street. But the demand for the writer,
the artist, is to be on the deserted side of the street,
clear of the collective. You've a far better view of what's
going on. You're not marching with the multitude. Is
it lonesome? It's lonesome at the start, but there are
attendant joys. You are doing what you are supposed
to be doing.

– Tom McIntyre (Gaelic footballer, poet,
playwright and writer)

KICKING MY BALL AROUND MY CHILDHOOD home is play.
It's a game. But it's important to realise that this isn't
sport. Something vital is missing. That something is the

other. The opponent. In that innocent game, I have no opponent. Not even a virtual opponent. Some would argue that the location and the set of tasks and skills I've challenged myself with could be construed as a virtual opponent, but I'm not buying that. I know what opponents are and my home isn't one of them. Nor am I my own opponent. I'm not playing against myself – although one can. Here I'm just playing. With a ball.

My home is the location of the game and sport needs a location – a place: pitch, court, track, course, pool ... whatever. John Bale says that 'Sports landscapes are often accumulations ... Just as each stadium has a builder, however, each landscape can be interpreted as having an "author" and a historical/economic context. Sport can therefore be seen as a "world of authored landscapes".' And I am the author of the landscape of my childhood game.

Sport also needs time (in the same way that literature or story needs time – sport and literature are temporal art forms) and I have that too. Thankfully, children are rich in time. In my game, I am more in *kairos* than *chronos*.

Sport also needs equipment – bat, stick, racket, gun (yes, gun), goals, and so on. I have these, too, in my ball and my feet (very often sports equipment is the body or, in the case of a hurley or tennis racket, an extension of the body).

This play has some of the elements of sport. Play itself is a prerequisite for sport. We *play* rugby, camogie, hockey, cricket (even though sometimes sport may appear more like work or war, it is, in fact, play). We play sport within a set of rules and regulations – and I have those too, even if I've codified the game myself and I may, at any point, change the rules.

But the lack of an opponent makes all the difference. Because there is no opponent, there is no *agôn* or struggle against an *other*.

Agôn is, of course, from where we get the word agony, which is the consequence of loss. And sport is, ultimately, about winning and losing (primarily losing, which is another reason that I see sport as a form of storytelling). My childhood football game in 1973 isn't about winning or losing. Even if I make a hash of my first kick, or (more agonisingly – drama in the third act has more substance, after all) my last kick, it doesn't matter. I'm playing for the sake of play, for the joy of it. I'm winning, no matter what happens.

I've never understood Sartre's comment that everything in football is complicated by the presence of the other team. It could be that in sport (with an *other* trying to best you) the purity of play and the instinct to play is convoluted into something else: something different.

Sport must have a struggle (and literature must have this too – the protagonist and antagonist) or it isn't sport. Sport, at its purest level, is me versus him, she versus her, us versus them. And because there is a them, there is an us and this us is the collective.

And because we are part of this collective, we are not alone. Even the solo runner or tennis player is part of such a collective. You are part of a collective, even if it isn't a sporting one, and it means that you're not alone.

Sport is all about not being alone, about the need to not feel alone and it's good at it.

Being part of a collective is attractive to us mammals. Mammals are pack or pod creatures. We're safe there and we know it. In today's society there are many such groupings: regional, political, religious, sexual, social. And one of the most common social collectives relates to sport. At times, the bloody thing seems ubiquitous.

Sport is also closely tied into community and identity – our sense of self, even our sense of self-worth. Which is why 90,000 people turned out to welcome the Limerick hurling team home in August 2018. Because of those hurlers, the people of Limerick valued more highly their identity, their community, themselves. And they wanted to thank the players for that gift.

As I kick my ball around my home in 1973, I too am part of a collective – and it's a collective of love (and all sport issues from love). I love having a ball at my feet, it fires my imagination. Every touch of it is vivid and intimate. I feel more alive here than I do anywhere else and many other children feel this fire, too. This is my collective on the Cork Road. Although I don't really know what I'm doing, my love of play and my love of sport, and my love of George Best and Manchester United are nurturing this play. I am alone, but I don't feel alone. I feel complete.

I've always felt somehow inside and yet at the same time outside of sport. Inside and outside the collective. Even when I was playing serious sport, I felt somehow different – and not in a good way. I wanted to belong and I wanted to feel that I belonged, but I couldn't quite manage it. I still can't.

In a way I was nowhere. And I've always felt (and still do) that I was nobody. That I didn't have an identity, an ego. I can say my name and who I am and describe my roots, and my life and my family but it's always been as if I were talking about somebody else and not myself. I always felt (even at moments of joy and glory, perhaps especially at moments of joy and glory) like I was outside looking in at my own life instead of being inside myself and looking out at the world.

I loved playing football for Mallow United. I loved being joined to the ball and I felt very much at home on the pitch. All the anxieties that beset my young inner life were swept away during play. It was literally an escape.

When I was playing, the ball at my feet, I also felt very much part of the team – I had a role, I was useful, I was valued. I was a vital piece of the jigsaw. There I was, truly and fully part of the collective. I belonged.

Somehow, I valued my existence on a football pitch more than on a hurling pitch. I think it may have had to do with my bond with the ball at my feet or a feeling of confidence. Maybe I could see myself as a footballer more than a hurler. Maybe it had something to do with my childhood game.

But before and after matches, I didn't feel comfortable with the other players. I didn't feel better than them (the opposite, in fact), but I did feel different. I felt like an outsider. During the game I was very much one of us, competing against them. I wanted that so badly. And sport did grant me that and I'm grateful for it. I've found it very rarely elsewhere.

When I was twenty-three, after a miserable few years when I eventually flunked out of college, I got a job in Cork City Library. My brother-in-law, the poet Tom McCarthy, wangled it for me somehow. That, and falling in love with a great woman, saved me and gave me a purpose for living that I'd lost. This renewed my love of the game and the ball, too.

I was living in a flat on John's Street, on the northside of Cork city and I was happy – for the first time in a long time. I was slowly shedding some of the miserable skin of college, sloughing off my failures, guilt and shame. I was regaining some of the light I had lost in my late teens and early twenties.

Picture this: a winter's Sunday morning. I'm sitting on the footpath by Murphy's Brewery in Blackpool waiting for the Mallow United football team bus to pick me up for a game in Cork city. I have my boots in a small plastic bag by my side. I have a close-cropped haircut and I'm wearing an old battered sheepskin jacket I am ridiculously fond of – it has the look of a Kerouac on the road, I'm convinced. I'm just sitting on the footpath, my back against the brewery wall.

One of the other players told me (years later) that when the bus pulled up, a teammate said: 'Jesus, would you look at the state of Coakley' and the others laughed. He thought I looked like a wino sitting there. I was that different from my teammates. I think I was a bit proud when he said that to me (I wanted to be different, I cultivated it, in a way), but I was also a bit sad. I didn't belong in the collective. Not really.

There's a photo of our team that year and there are thirteen men in it (eleven players and two managers). Every one of them is looking at the camera. I am looking down. All of them are smiling – except me. I am frowning. I'm at the edge of the team. Almost all of the players have long hair (the fashion at the time). I don't. It's no coincidence I'm on the edge of the photo and not nearer the middle.

Even when I was playing hurling for UCC and winning Fitzgibbon Cups and our coach, the great Canon Michael O'Brien, trusted me to do a job for the team year after year. Even then, I didn't fully feel part of it or worthy of it. I loved my teammates and I loved the hurling and I loved winning, but it was always like this was happening to someone else, not me.

None of the players in any of the many teams I played on was at my wedding in 1991 – I've often speculated why that was. I guess that, outside the pitch, I wasn't connected enough with them – however much I wanted to be.

This sporting theme of being inside/outside the collective is wonderfully shown in the play *The Man from Clare* (1962), by John B. Keane. Keane understood sport very well and he understood that fiction contains a deeper truth than facts.

The main character in the play is Padraic O'Dea – the eponymous man from Clare in the title. He is a footballer and the hero of the Cuas team. Cuas are beaten in a match in Kerry but the important element of the game is that Padraic did not play well, he was eclipsed by a younger player, Jim, and he comes to the realisation that he is no longer physically capable of being the hero. Age has defeated him and he has an existential crisis, his identity having been stripped off his back like a football jersey after a game. He attempts suicide by drowning but can't go through with it and on his return from the water he comes across a barn where Jim and the other players are dancing and carousing with some local girls. This pivotal scene of the play sees a dishevelled Padraic (failed footballer, failed suicide) looking through a gap in the barn wall at the collective merriment and joy and belonging going on inside. It's a wonderful visual image of an outsider looking on in grief at those who are still buoyant and safe inside the collective.

Now, I wonder if my feeling of not belonging in the sporting collective wasn't just a manifestation of introversion or social anxiety or youthful isolation or angst or a lack of direction. But I wonder too if it was the writer in me. As a writer, I think one has to be both inside and outside the collective, the society, the norm.

There's a duality, which is disconcerting if one isn't aware of it and accepting of it.

I think this duality is now standing to me as I try to write, and to write about sport – that sense of being an outsider. Tom McIntyre asks if it's lonesome. Yes, it's lonesome, sometimes – ask any writer. Feeling lonesome hurts, and it did hurt me a lot over the years. I want to belong; I want to be inside.

When McIntyre says: 'But the demand for the writer, the artist, is to be on the deserted side of the street, clear of the collective' he is implying you can't be part of the sports collective if you are a writer. You can't have it both ways.

I hope he's wrong, because that's exactly what I want.

Simon Barnes writes about how, on an afternoon before a European Championship football game between England and Portugal in Lisbon, he's in a bar with some English fans. At the time he was the chief sportswriter for *The Times*.

He describes the fans as the type of men that he would cross the M25 to avoid – shaven heads, tattoos, bellies. But he also admits (despite his own nerves about the game) that they care more about the result than he does. He hates them for that. And yet there they all are, together, in a Lisbon bar, drinking beer, dreading and looking forward to the same game.

Barnes talks down the fans (one of them orders '*dos* beers') while he is reading Fernando Pessoa's masterpiece *The Book of Disquiet*. He is feeling superior, but he's also aware of the feeling. He's also intoxicated by the fact that, on the following day, his words will be on the front page of *The Times*.

He feels very different from the players, the Beckhams and Rooneys too. He admits that they possess far greater 'intellectual depth' than he does. They can compute dynamics of spin and curve and the probabilities of human bodies colliding at high speed. Abilities far more important, he's implying, than appreciating Pessoa's beautiful prose.

Barnes is also aware of the fact that Beckham is the creator of tales while he, a mere writer, is [only] the teller. He says 'there's a lifetime of difference here [between himself and Beckham]: and with it, enough shame and glory to last a lifetime of words'. The writer Mike McCormack once said the engineers make the world but the writers only describe what's been made. In sport the players are the real storytellers, the sportswriters just translate the stories into words.

Perhaps that feeling of being different and the knowledge of it is key to being an effective writer. And perhaps I should embrace it, as I now try to make sense of sport in my own texts.

I workshopped a version of this essay in Dublin in 2019 and the poet and essayist Emily Cooper pointed out a different way to look at the issue. Instead of feeling caught between two stools (literature and sport), she said, maybe you have two stools to stand on and maybe two are better than one? The poetic simplicity of her thinking and perspective was one of the highlights of the week's workshop and I decided to take her advice.

In a way, Barnes – (like me) a writer and a football fan – is both inside and outside his collective. Inside it, caring about the result, being nervous, drinking beer in a bar in the afternoon with other fans. Outside it, detached from the other fans, reading Pessoa and writing something that will be on the front page of *The Times* the following day.

And isn't it great to have two viewpoints instead of one?

When I go to Cork or Mallow or Munster or Ireland or Manchester United games, I'm not among people I'd cross the N20 to avoid. I like these people, who are mostly men. I'm happy to be among them in the same collective. But I don't feel like them.

If I were on a train or in a pub, I probably wouldn't have much to say to them (Cork hurling fans, let's say), once we'd exhausted sporting talk. But here we are, getting ready to cheer on the same team, and I'm in the multitude, on the crowded side of the street. Our feet, as the author Claire Keegan says, have brought us to the place where we want to be: to our object of desire.

I'm nervous and they're nervous. I love Cork hurling and they love Cork hurling – perhaps more than me. I know hurling and they know hurling – perhaps better than me. They live for these moments, when sport lifts them into the light, as do I. They feel a sense of rightness and belonging, that they *should be* here and now and doing this. And I feel that rightness too.

Sport is full of contradictions – in fact sport is one big contradiction: sport is something trivial that we have to take very seriously. And here I am: in a collective with people I don't really know (apart from a few friends) and with whom I share less than I'd like to. I'm inside and I'm outside the collective. I'm in the wood and among the trees. I'm part of the multitude and I'm on the deserted side of the street.

It's where I need to be, if I'm going to write about it all.

David Foster Wallace was born in 1962 – a year after me – and he was the archetypal outsider/insider. When he taught at Illinois State University in the town of Normal (which is funny when you think about it), he lived in a nearby town, preferring the company of townspeople to the university academics in Normal.

Wallace was anxious and depressed as a child but he loved to play tennis; it allowed him to be competitive and to be part of a collective. It helped him forget who he was and how alone he was. When he was twelve he won a prize for poetry and used the $50 to pay for tennis camp. He became a very good tennis player, ranked in the junior Midwest division.

Wallace got sport and he got writing. Good writing, he said, should help its readers to 'become less alone inside'. And by being less alone, we become more joined to the collective.

Wallace used tennis in his major novel *Infinite Jest*: it hinges around the sport. One of its primary locations is the Enfield Tennis Academy (ETA), and its protagonist (sort of) is Hal Incandenza, who is training to be a top junior player there. ETA is run by Incandenza's (broken) family, but Hal is broken too. He has an eidetic memory and has memorised the *Oxford English Dictionary* word for word. He smokes marijuana obsessively and has a mental breakdown. Tennis cannot save him.

Wallace's sports writing is stellar. When exploring the inarticulation of most sports autobiographies, he said that the cruel paradox of sport is that 'we, the spectators [a word I dislike because of its passivity] who are not divinely gifted as athletes, are the only ones able to see, articulate and animate the experience of the gift we are denied. And those who receive and act out the gift of athletic genius must, perforce, be blind and dumb about it – and not because blindness and dumbness are the price of the gift, but because they are its essence.'

These great sportspeople, at the crucial moment of the game, are able to cut off every force of distraction and what Wallace called the 'Iago-like voice of the self'. This is one of the gifts they have that separates them from us normal people. That is the collective of the player and it's a place of deafness, blindness and dumbness – a place beyond words.

We, the fans, are in a different (but related) collective. We look on and enter the game empathically, but we also remain outside and separate from it. Our collective – in the crowd – is a place of watching and listening and chatter.

Just as tennis could not save Hal Incandenza, it could not save David Foster Wallace – not even the thought of living in the same world as a Federer. Although Wallace gloried in the beauty of great athletes he also envied it. He thought of greatness in sport as something he was denied.

Even though Michael Jordan hung in the air like a Chagall bride, even though Sampras defied Euclid. Even though, to paraphrase Wallace, sport allowed humans to carve out exemptions from physical laws and to create a transcendent beauty that made God manifest in man. It wasn't enough.

David Foster Wallace committed suicide on 12 September 2008, aged forty-six.

So, mine is a life spent in and out of various sporting collectives on and off the pitches, tracks and courses. It isn't uncommon.

A Manchester United supporter from the age of seven when United won the European Cup and George Best strode across my world – a God. A Cork supporter, especially since my brother Dermot starred on the Cork Minor hurling team when I was ten and my father brought me to matches. A Mallow hurling supporter at a time when Mallow's Senior team was outstanding.

As a GAA player, various underage teams for Mallow, Under 12 in hurling and Gaelic football, Under 14 and Under 16 too. In secondary school, at St Colman's College, a member of various hurling and Gaelic football teams, Under 14½, Under 15½, then Under 17 (Dean Ryan Cup in hurling), then Senior hurling and Gaelic football (Dr Harty Cup (Munster) and Dr Croke Cup (All-Ireland) in the case of hurling).

Cork Minor, Cork Under 21, UCC Senior Hurling (for four years), Combined University teams. Minor, Under 21 and Senior for my home club, Mallow (Senior really being Intermediate, which I played for thirteen years). Senior football for Mallow United for maybe seven or eight years.

I played on many teams (some serious) from the ages of eleven to thirty. I've probably forgotten many of them. I was part of so many collectives on the pitch and so many others off the pitch. I played golf in my thirties, forties and fifties, mostly not serious golf nor as part of teams but I did play in championships and competitions and I was a member of a club – so I was embedded inside that specific local collective and the overall golfer one, too. When I was fifty or fifty-one I lost my nerve in a golf team event in Galway (which I'll describe later) and I called a halt – that was that: it would only be play and not competitive sport from now on, but that involves collectives, too.

All those sporting collectives, down through the years. Did I feel comfortable within them? Not always. But I was inside them, I was welcomed in, I wanted to be there. Some people aren't so lucky and look in, longingly (like Padraic O'Dea in *The Man from Clare*) from the outside.

A few years after that final competitive game of golf – my last act as a sportsman – I began writing. At first, I didn't know how I'd manage to write or what about, but I figured it out soon enough. I'd given up sport as a player – or rather it had spat me out – but, before long, I was trying to find it again as a writer.

I replaced the fervour of physical play with the fervour of the good sentence, the good review, the acceptance email by an editor, the approbation of readers and peers. So I became part of literary collectives. First, in an MA in creative writing class, then editing a journal with other writers, then performing at literary events and being known as a writer. Different writers' groups, collectives of writers who meet every so often, then in a group of writers working with a publisher and then as a published author – that's a collective too, of sorts.

But do I feel at home in any of these collectives? I did feel part of my MA class; there we were, all aspiring writers, learning, sharing the insecurities and pressures and travails that come with a serious creative writing course and putting ourselves out there. And I do feel comfortable with my writing groups – we have become friends, so that helps. I care about them. But in a group of writers, say at a book launch or a reading, I'll feel the old niggling spider crawling under my skin: *unworthy, different, uncomfortable*. It's pestering and pushing me to leave, to run away and get safely home.

Alcohol helps but I'm so nervous around these literary people that I don't feel safe enough to get drunk enough to feel comfortable in their various collective companies.

As a writer among writers I *am* in that collective. I chose to write and they chose to write (and not many people are crazy enough to make such an ill-advised choice) so there is a sameness among us and a shared identity.

I'm doing what I'm supposed to be doing, now, which is writing. And there are attendant joys, such as the sense of purpose on a dark November morning heading to my desk with a cup of tea; the sight of my name on a book cover on a shelf; my name under a newspaper headline; or a stranger sending me an email saying my writing moved them.

I'm doing what I'm supposed to be doing now and I was doing what I was supposed to be doing when I was young: playing sport on teams, joyful in the collective.

GIVING VOICE TO MY
OWN ASTONISHMENT

This is a book that no one will like, not intellectuals, who aren't interested in football, or football lovers, who will find it too intellectual. But I had to write it, I didn't want to break the fine thread that still connects me to the world.

– *Football*, Jean-Philippe Touissaint

I N July 2019 Fintan O'Toole expressed his anger in *The Irish Times* that the plan to develop Parnell Square as a cultural hub had been scrapped by Dublin City Council. He contrasted this with the co-funding by the Irish government of the 2026 Ryder Cup in Adare Manor.

His opening line in the piece was: 'Could we not just abolish culture and call it sport? A bit extreme, I know.' Later down the article he wrote: 'Perhaps if we called novelists golfers and painters jockeys and musicians footballers, and organised poets into country teams with their own jerseys we might get somewhere.'

What struck me about the article was not so much O'Toole's attack on the 'godawful philistinism and hypocrisy of a state that names bridges and naval vessels after dead artists but refuses to invest seriously in the culture from which living ones emerge'. I share that anger and support his criticism.

The jarring note in the piece was that O'Toole did not appear to consider sport as culture. Not even a sport like hurling, which dates back 3,000 years into Irish prehistory and is embedded in our mythology. Is O'Toole suggesting that sport cannot be considered as important as other aspects of culture? Is he saying that sport cannot be considered a form of art?

I don't think he is saying that.

My first reaction to the piece was to defend sport against a perceived intellectual attack and this reflects more on me than it does on O'Toole. The fact is that many Irish sportswriters and intellectuals who love sport have perceived a snobbery (intellectual or otherwise) towards sport by 'Official Ireland' or 'Intellectual Ireland'. But I have never personally experienced that snobbery. Nor has anybody I've read or listened to convinced me of that snobbery.

Of course some writers and intellectuals do look down on sport, as some sports fans do look down on literature. But there is a difference between some intellectuals and many intellectuals being snobbish about sport.

There are snobberies in all walks of life. There are snobberies within sport, too. Some fans of hurling look down on Gaelic football. Some fans of rugby look down on football. Some fans of tennis look down on squash. Everybody looks down on golf.

But that doesn't say anything about Gaelic football, football, squash or golf – it says something about the fans who look down on them.

Nor is this specifically an 'Irish problem'.

Simon Barnes writes about the snobbery that intellectuals display towards sport. He contrasts attitudes towards sex and sport. Sex and sport have this in common: stupid people like them both. The difference is that clever people can also enjoy sex without forfeiting their right to be considered clever. But a clever person who says they enjoy sport will be considered less clever as a result (or so he claims).

He admired the confidence of A.S. Byatt, the English novelist and poet who admitted she only watched live sport and 24-hour digital news on television. 'Everything else is too slow,' she said, memorably, 'telling you things you already know.' To Barnes, this was both brave and a tease. Her reputation for great cleverness meant she could get away with it. The tease was that if one claims to like sport, one is knowingly stepping away from the intellectual side of life. This, Barnes says, is why so many politicians claim to be football fans: it makes them seem like 'good ordinary people'. We don't want to be governed by anyone too clever, and so Tony Blair maintained he was a big Newcastle United fan – in an attempt to make himself more loveable, more one of us, more part of our collective.

But, according to Barnes, for an intellectual to appear really clever, it's not enough to dislike sport; you have to despise sport.

I don't think that Barnes proves his point. The sportswriter doth protest too much, methinks.

And when I read of such perceived snobbery, I wonder sometimes if there is an inferiority complex at play. I say that because sometimes when I write about sport, I can see such an inferiority complex in action within me.

I remember the writer Colm Tóibín once discussing why the portrayal of women characters in his books is so good. He said that when he was a child he would leave the living room, where men were talking about hurling, and go into the kitchen, where women were talking about clothes. To me, this isn't a sign of snobbery from Tóibín, it's just that he preferred to hear about clothes and to listen to women talk. He identified more with it, it interested him more, there was more truth in it for him.

Some people who don't know sport only see its outward physical manifestation and this lessens it for them in relation to other arts, which they perceive as being more based on the intellect and on the senses.

Another reason for alienation by some people is sport's popularity and near-ubiquity in media and broadcasting. In 2019 a writer friend asked me why sport had a section on every news bulletin; and why was it entitled to two slots in the RTÉ radio news programme *Morning Ireland* while the arts barely get a mention? If I were averse to sport I'd be just as angry, but, of course, the reason for the dominance is sport's popularity and the high place it holds in so many hearts – a place far higher than 'the arts' do. Sport, to me, is among the arts, but my friend doesn't believe that.

When my book *The First Sunday in September* came out, a friend told me that many of his gay friends disliked sport. Some of their fathers (perhaps perceiving a lack of 'manliness' in them) tried to force them into contact sports, to 'toughen them up'. So, for them, sport represents a kind of antipathy of who they are. Sport is, in some ways, a mirror held up to them, representing their failure to be the kind of sons their fathers desired. No wonder they hate it.

Other writers have spoken to me about their aversion to sport because they were forced to play sport as children against their will. This is what also led to George Orwell's hatred of sport, in his case at public school.

Other 'non-sporting' friends, when discussing this book, also told me of the kind of failure they felt in not being adept at or even interested in sport. How their families were divided into the sporty and the non-sporty. How they regretted that they were not among the sporty ones. How they were poor when it came to the currency that sport bestows in society, even within families. It was their lot to be the nerdy ones and it was a lesser lot – even the word 'nerd' carries its own pejorative baggage.

Again, I understand such feelings, but any resulting antipathy towards sport seems to me to be a type of transference and perhaps a reductive way of looking at it.

But it certainly isn't snobbery.

The most common question journalists ask me is why sport doesn't feature more in the canon of Irish literature, Irish fiction in particular.

And the question isn't only being asked by sportswriters.

Those writing and broadcasting on literature and culture ask it too. And they often point out that such a dearth of sport in fiction doesn't occur in the United States (John Updike, Norman Mailer, F. Scott Fitzgerald, Philip Roth, Don DeLillo, Richard Ford, Stephen King, David Foster Wallace, Chad Harbach, inter alia) or in the UK (P.G. Wodehouse, Catherine Cookson, David Storey, David Peace, Philip Kerr, Nick Hornby, John King, Ross Raisin, Nathan Leamon, inter alia). So why is it the case for Ireland (with some recent exceptions by Joseph O'Neill, Donal Ryan, Paul Howard, Patrick Osborne, Eimear Ryan, Rónán Hession and Adrian Duncan)?

The truth is that I don't know that answer to that question, much as I have thought about it. Although I do know how difficult it is to write a sports novel and how difficult it is to have it published.

First of all, on the supply side, looking at fiction writers who might consider writing such a novel, I estimate that if one surveyed a hundred random and representative Irish fiction writers, fewer than ten of them would be interested enough in sport to write a novel based around it. You have to really care about something to spend three or four years engrossed in it. When I asked Joseph O'Neill why he picked cricket as the sport in *Netherland*, he told me it was because he was obsessed with the game. When I asked Adrian Duncan why he wrote about football in *Midfield Dynamo*, he said it was because he found it beautiful.

Writing a novel is a serious investment and a serious undertaking. It isn't so much a case of writing what you know about (most crime writers don't know how to murder people) so much as writing about what you care about.

Another obstacle on the supply side is what John McGahern

called 'the double artifice'. Writing and reading work by artifice, by a kind of pretence. The words 'art' and 'artifice' have the same roots. When we read a novel, we have to put aside the fact (which we rationally know to be true) that what we are reading is completely false; it was dreamed up in the mind of a writer somewhere and sometime and then put down on paper using words arrayed in a complex and very strict set of rules and regulations which have to do with syntax, punctuation and grammar. In effect the writer is attempting to bring her characters to life on the page by a kind of Frankensteinian magic.

And she is also selecting a very precise narrative to include in the novel, based on ideas about form and story that are quite old and prescribed. This imposition, Donal Ryan says, is 'an unnatural act' but as readers we have to 'forget' all this and delve into the world and the people on the pages as though they are true. We have to fool ourselves completely for writing to work, for us to believe the characters are alive. And we do this willingly – we must for writing to function – but it takes a certain amount of self-deception to experience the emotion we can draw out of the text.

When we go to the theatre, we know that we are looking at actors on a stage pretending to be characters in a book or play. It's a stage in a theatre, not a bedroom or a living room in a house. The people on the stage are 'players' in a 'play' – they are 'playing' at being these characters using the characters' voices, acting their actions. We, the audience (the fans) agree to be deceived in this way – it's how art works. We agree to 'play' along; we want to; we have to, in order for us to feel what we want to feel as the tension and drama unfold on the stage so that we can be inside it.

The same self-deception happens in sport. Those outside

sport, looking on, see (in rugby for example) a certain crazy and indiscriminate display of brutality. Thirty (mostly huge) players are apparently chasing a ball on a muddy field and trying to carry this ball over the end-line of their opponents. They are committing physical violence against each other to gain possession of the ball – carrying out acts that, on the street, would be classified as assault causing serious harm and would lead to jail sentences. There are some rules at play, apparently, none of which seem to make any sense. From time to time the bigger players form themselves into a kind of crouching centipede and push against the opposition and the ball is thrown underneath them. When the ball crosses the sideline the same players form two lines and the ball is thrown above them. The fact that millions of people are engrossed by this violent, brutal farce makes no sense at all.

Those inside rugby, on the contrary, see a beautiful and well-ordered, complex and utterly absorbing drama and they manage this by unseeing what I have just described. It's another form of self-deception, which they willingly undergo to experience emotion. For sport to function, this artifice must take place.

Now, for a writer to manage such artifice (to fool the reader in some ways) and to ensure the reader fully enters the false world of the novel, takes craft and rigour. But in sports fiction the reader also has to engage in a second level of self-deception inside the first one, to make the sporting artifice also work. Both types of artifice have to function simultaneously to infuse the necessary life into the subject (as McGahern put it). And this is very difficult to manage.

But on the demand side there are further challenges.

First of all, to get a book published, you have to convince commissioning editors and publishing houses that they want it.

Again, if you take a hundred random editors, how many of them want to edit a book rooted in sport? Again, I'm going to say a maximum of ten. In one publishing house to which I submitted *The First Sunday in September* the editor liked the stories but told me that when he was young and there was football in school, he was the football. His aversion to sport would make it very difficult for him to work with a sports novel.

Then there's the fact that about 80 per cent of novels are read by women and most sports fans are men. When Ross Raisin wrote *A Natural* – a brilliant sports novel about a gay professional footballer in England – he and the publisher of his first two novels, Penguin, saw the book differently and the novel went on submission. Other publishers were quite upfront about saying (and this is a quote from Ross from a *Guardian* piece): 'We don't know how to sell it to women because it's about football, but at the same time we don't know how we can sell it to football supporters because it's got a gay in it.' Thankfully the book was published by Jonathan Cape in 2017.

Ross felt that the attitude of some publishers towards the book was unsurprising. He said: 'But I'm interested in how the book is received because it's not a book for men, it's not a book for football supporters, it's a book for readers. You can write fiction that is searching and empathetically complicated about any subject.' He is drawn to situations with 'a dead crust of opinion around them'.

The dead crust of opinion aside, I understand where the publishers were coming from. Publishing is a business and businesses deal in the bottom line – profit. And I'm not sure how well sports fiction sells in Ireland and the UK, even books written as brilliantly as Ross Raisin's.

Select another representative hundred die-hard football fans at a game – these will be mostly young men. How many of them are interested in reading a book like *A Natural*? Ten? Maybe that's being optimistic.

None of this is snobbery, by the way. Not the attitude of the writers nor the readers, editors or publishers. The vast majority of writers and readers and editors and publishers are just not interested in sports fiction. Which, to people like me (and perhaps you) may seem incredible. But there it is.

It's not necessary to have played sport to write compellingly about it.

My favourite sports novel is *The Throwback Special* by Chris Bachelder and I don't know if Chris played American football. I suspect he didn't, but it doesn't matter. What matters is that the game astonishes him and the specific play the novel revolves around (a Monday night game in 1985 when the New York Giants linebacker Lawrence Taylor ended the playing career of the Washington Redskins quarterback Joe Theismann with a horrific tackle) astonishes him. The book isn't about American football, that tackle or even sport. The book is about what we lose and gain when we enter middle age. The men in the book, as Bachelder says, have 'reached a point when they see what their lives are going to become for better or worse'. The book is about what they do with that knowledge – what we all do with that knowledge.

Likewise *A Natural* isn't about football, it's about identity and shame and love.

In the *Behind The Lines* podcast in 2021, Donal Ryan, who

consistently threads hurling into his novels and short stories, said: 'You have to be free as a writer, you have to be able to write any type of character sympathetically and properly and do your homework.' But, he adds, having been a fan since his childhood: 'When it comes to sport, I've been doing my homework my whole life.'

To make sport matter to readers in fiction, it has to matter in life for the writer. It does for Donal Ryan and Ross Raisin and it did for John McGahern and John B. Keane and David Foster Wallace.

In her book *The Writing Life*, the American Pulitzer Prize-winning writer Annie Dillard summed it up best about what we should write:

> Why do you never find anything written about that idiosyncratic thought you advert to, about your fascination with something no one else understands? Because it is up to you. There is something you find interesting, for a reason hard to explain. It is hard to explain because you have never read it on any page; there you begin. You were made and set here to give voice to this; your own astonishment.

PART 4

DARK PASSIONS

Men who go into competition with the world are broken into fragments by the world, and it is such men we love to analyse. But men who do not go into competition with the world remain intact, and these men we cannot analyse. They are always contented men, with modest ambitions.

– 'The End of a Good Man', Seán Ó Faoláin

I was at the Munster hurling final in 2010. A child was sitting beside me with his father. The boy was eight or nine. Not long after the beginning of the match, the father and son changed places and I realised that it was because of me. Something I'd said, or maybe shouted or sworn, the look in my eyes, my rigid body language or the tone of my voice, had frightened the child.

They didn't return to their seats after half time – the father must have found a safer place in the stadium for his boy to watch the game – and the empty seats were an admonishment all second half. I felt ashamed.

At another game, some years previously, an opposition player was sent off for striking a Cork player and as he was walking off the field I shouted (in anger) something like: 'That's the fucking place for him, he should be in jail, anyway.' I was referring to a rumour I'd heard that the same player had recently assaulted a man who was subsequently hospitalised.

I had no idea if the rumour about the player was true or not. It probably wasn't and even if it were true, should I have made that comment? Of course not, this is just a game. Players strike each other all the time in hurling and they shouldn't, but if one is sent off does he deserve to have his name blackened publicly by an angry idiot who knows nothing about him?

And yet, even now, while I am in the process of writing this book, when I am very conscious of my emotions and actions during games, I find myself acting in ways of which I'm not proud. Shouting at referees, shouting at opposition players, complaining about bad wides or bad fouls (fouls only on 'my' players). Petulantly begrudging the team that beats Mallow, Cork, Munster, Ireland, or Manchester United their win. I tell myself before the game to be the fan and not the fanatic, that everybody has a right to be there, that everybody is doing the best they can, that I am privileged to even be present, that this is a joyful occasion.

I tell myself to calm down, that it's 'only' a game.

But I can't.

I know that, in a way, some of this objectionable behaviour is a kind of safety in numbers idiocy. When we are present in a crowd and when groupthink happens, we lose some of our individual inhibitions and become part of a more homogenous unit.

Everett Dean Martin in his book *The Behavior of Crowds: A Psychological Study* says: 'I know of nothing which today so menaces not only the values of civilization, but also ... the achievement of personality and true knowledge of self, as the growing habit of behaving as crowds.' And sport facilitates such menaces because it is perhaps society's main enabler of crowds, week-in and week-out, in highly charged and testosterone-laden stadiums and bars.

The usual macho social stigmas that prevent men from expressing their emotions are absent within the catalytic invocation of a sports crowd. And these emotions are heightened when you add the cocktail of alcohol and gambling and the mob mentality that men use to amplify their passion during games. I was bringing anger to the game when the father moved his child away, but others bring racism, sectarianism, nationalism, violence, homophobia and sexism – all manner of toxic masculine behaviour.

The crowd facilitates this behaviour. To be part of a collective, we have to obey the rules of the collective – we have to conform. We want to be part of the group, to have the safety in numbers and the anonymity it bestows. I think this is also one of the attractions of social media. But what if the group is shouting homophobic chants at one of the opposition players? We might not shout, ourselves, or we might, but we certainly won't go against the grain and criticise others for it.

A friend of mine from Belfast told me about being at a football match in Windsor Park watching Northern Ireland play. He's a big fan of the team. Windsor Park is a very Loyalist grounds but my friend is a Nationalist. Suddenly all the fans around him started singing: 'If you hate the Fenian bastards clap your hands.' And everybody would clap their hands three times between each chant. So my friend had to either refuse to conform – perhaps identifying himself as a Fenian bastard. Or else he had to admit to hating himself by clapping his hands.

He was telling me this over a pint. As usual we were talking about sport.

'What did you do?' I asked, delighted with his dilemma.

'I pulled my hands together, as if I were clapping,' he said. 'But at the last second my hands didn't touch, so I didn't actually clap.'

He thought this was a very clever solution to a deeply moral dilemma. I had to agree. It was Jesuitical.

He could appear to be part of the collective of fans – in one sense he was part of them, as a Northern Ireland football supporter – but without denying his real collective, the Nationalist people of the North.

But the fact that he and I were laughing about this 'sporting' tribal sectarianism, and were so accepting of it, says a lot too.

In attending a Donald Trump rally in 2016, George Saunders noted a distinct deterioration of crowd behaviour during the actual event, once Trump had appeared. Beforehand, Saunders was able to chat to Trump supporters; they didn't share his values but they were moderate in how they disagreed with him. But during the event and afterwards, the need to conform, to collectively act out the nastiness of Trump, was too strong and they regressed to the lowest, most brutish common denominator. I think this happens during games, too. The passion and the need to be part of the supporters' group is so strong that everyone there worsens to the basest of its characteristics – it becomes more and more extreme.

I would never shout at the referee or opponent players before a game (I would certainly never shout at anybody at a play or concert), but I feel entitled to do it during a match. The perceived approbation of those around me when I do shout strengthens my anger and diminishes my usual balance.

The US sociologist Jay Coakley writes that ethical problems and deviance exist in sport because those involved (players or fans) commit themselves without 'question or reservation' to the normative guidelines apparent in the sport. And if the normative guidelines are sectarianism or racism (or cheating), then the fan or player will commit himself blindly to such conformity in the group.

Sport is a double-edged sword. It facilitates us men to both feel great emotion and to express it – the kinds of emotion I earlier described my father experiencing in Kent Station in 1979. Where else will you see so many men unashamedly weep tears of joy except at a match where their county or club wins an All-Ireland final or a Premier League title? Where else will you see the sideline hugs and kisses of mothers and fathers and loved ones?

We want this emotional release; we seek it out. We crave it, like we crave our tears at tear-jerker films, like we crave our fear at horror films, like we crave our sense of thrill and excitement during thrillers. But very often we cannot control our emotions in these situations. My own father had to stop going to games because he used to become dangerously excited and uncontrollably angry. This is true of many men. I'm fully aware of all this when I experience it or witness it in others, yet I still get angry and frustrated and behave in petty and ignominious ways at sporting events.

If people who knew me outside of sport saw me in these situations, saw how their gentle, mild-mannered friend behaves in a crowd – or even in front of the TV – they would be shocked. And, even when I am well-behaved in my actions, inside me the anger, bitterness and joylessness of my feelings are swirling around like a toxic sludge.

I'm generally a laid-back, amiable person. I'm not given to hate or violence. But there is anger inside me. I am angry about Putin's invasion of Ukraine and climate change denial and all sorts of issues. I'm also probably angry about aspects of my own life. For the most part, I am well able to keep my anger in check, but sport is one of the few areas in my life where the anger can be pried loose. And I do let it loose; in fact I'm not sure I can stop it.

The obvious question arises: if I cannot control this behaviour, this level of negative emotion, would I be better off without sport altogether? Would all those who go to games, who are obsessed by sport, be better off without it?

The Canadian psychologist Robert J. Vallerand has shown that two different types of passion exist in sport: one associated with adaptive outcomes (the sharing of positive experiences with fellow fans) and the other with maladaptive ones (behaving badly at games, or – an extreme example – the murder of Colombian defender Andres Escobar for scoring an own goal against the

USA in 1994. This is called the Dualistic Model of Passion and in 2008 Vallerand and other researchers tested it on sports fans (football fans, to be exact).

Vallerand defines passion as a 'strong inclination towards an activity that individuals like (or even love), that they value (and thus find important), and in which they invest time and energy'. Any fan will recognise that definition as applying to them. I hope you can recognise it in some aspect of your life.

Such a passion then serves to define the person, so that those who have a passion for supporting their team do not merely watch football, they *are* 'Manchester City' or 'Ireland' or 'Mourneabbey'. Cheering for one's team indirectly entails cheering for the self. Our teams are part of our identity – they are part of who we are.

This internalisation, according to the Dualistic Model of Passion, leads to two distinct types of passion. *Harmonious passion* results from an autonomous internalisation of the activity/ sport into the person's identity when we freely accept the sport as important for us – without contingencies, but with volition. That is, there is no uncontrollable urge to engage in the sport. The passionate activity is important for us, but it remains in harmony with other aspects of our lives. With harmonious passion, little conflict is expected with other activities in the person's life, with minimal negative impact in other life areas such as relationships, work and self-care.

In contrast, *obsessive passion* refers to an uncontrollable urge to engage in the activity that one loves – one cannot help but do it. This is because our feelings of social acceptance or self-esteem are inextricably linked to the activity/sport, or because the excitement we derive from it becomes uncontrollable. This leads to a 'rigid engagement and persistence' towards the passionate activity/sport, even when we should not do it, or when it is damaging to us or interferes with our lives. The activity/sport eventually comes to occupy disproportionate space in our identity and to cause conflict with other life activities. In other words, you could be with your partner and your children instead of at a game with your mates. You could be spending your money on family necessities instead of a Sky Sports subscription or betting on sport. You could have bought a new car instead of heading off to Italia '90 having taken out a Credit Union loan.

Needless to say, Vallerand found the presence of obsessive passion among the football fans in his studies. But anybody who has ever been present at a local derby or a tense game could have told him that. My friend in Windsor Park could have, for sure. We have all witnessed such dark passions.

At a football match in Turner's Cross in Cork in 1990, Ireland were beating England 4–1. The crowd around me on the terrace was ebullient. One man shouted, 'Come on Ireland, we got five at Brighton.' He was referring to the bombing of the Grand hotel in Brighton in 1984 when five people were murdered by the IRA. People chuckled and smiled at the comment. Celebrating murder is what passes for humour when teams are winning, but when teams are losing, or the game is in the balance, edges become sharper and barbs more vicious.

The opening of emotional dams allows the flow in both directions. Yes, there are the tears of joy at being rejoined again with those whom we have lost. The kissing of victorious players by loved ones. But sport also facilitates and normalises the worst excesses of human behaviour. And, because we are caught up in the crowd, we accept this. *It's only a bit of craic, only a bit of banter. Man up and don't be a fucking snowflake. What's the harm in a bit of queer chanting, it's only to put the player off? What's the harm in a bit of a kicking, they are all fucking cunts, aren't they?*

In sport, these behaviours flow as freely and as unquestioned as the millions of euro given by cash-strapped sports fanatics to multinational alcohol corporations, multinational betting companies, multinational media outlets, multinational sports associations, corrupt and nationalistic sports associations and multinational sports franchises.

The fact that I support Manchester United means that I have experienced great joy over the years, when 'my' team has been successful – in other words, when I have been successful.

But does my affection for Manchester United mean that I must also hate Liverpool? I don't think it does and I know (some) United fans who are okay with Liverpool and Manchester City and other rival teams. But I'm not okay with Liverpool and I think it's not too strong for me to say that I do hate Liverpool. I can't bear to see them win.

Last weekend, when I saw that Liverpool were losing to Crystal Palace I was delighted. When I found out they had come back to win, I was annoyed. My particular animus with Liverpool goes back to a time in my youth when their dominance of British and European football coincided with United's struggles to avoid relegation, so I do understand it, but that was decades ago.

Good friends of mine follow Liverpool Football Club. It is a deep element of their identity, how they see themselves. They have passed this love – let's call it what it is – on to their children. And, although I love my friends and their children and I wish them nothing but joy and happiness, I would have been happy to see them deprived of their bliss at the 2020 Premier League title – their first in twenty-nine years. I was delighted when Steven Gerrard made his famous slip in Stamford Bridge in April 2014, gifting Manchester City the title. I smile even now, eight years later, thinking of it. And I know how heartbreaking that was for my friends. But I'm perfectly happy for them to endure such heartbreak.

Isn't it time to let my hatred of Liverpool go? Now that I am aware of it and 'in full control' of my emotions, surely now would be a good time. Klopp isn't a bad guy, I was quite fond of him at Dortmund. What's not to love about the stunning beauty of Mohamed Salah on the ball? As Sally Rooney pointed out in her 2017 *Guardian* piece: 'For me, watching Mohamed Salah play football is not unlike staring up at the stars and contemplating the vastness of the universe: it makes my own life seem nice and small.' Why should I care if one dislikeable billionaire fiefdom franchise wins the league over another?

And think of the joy, think of the tears and the kisses, of the pure bliss of the Liverpool fans, some of whom I love.

But I won't let my hatred go. Not a hope.

I don't want to hate Liverpool or to wish them ill. But the 'rigid engagement and persistence' of my passionate activity (my wish for Liverpool to lose) is too strong. My wish to change is puny and irrelevant; my passionate activity is uncontrollable.

W ou le souvenir d'enfance (*W, or the Memory of Childhood*) is a novel by Georges Perec, published in 1975. It's semi-autobiographical in the sense that it features a child partly based on Perec's life story – he was a childhood evacuee from France during the

Second World War. In the novel the child is shipwrecked and washed up on a remote island, W. The purpose of the island is sport. That is, everybody on the island is devoted and dedicated to sport – there is nothing else. So, it's a Utopia – what could be more perfect, a place where there is only sport? That's every sports fan's dream, isn't it?

All the children on the island are being prepared for sport, all the able-bodied adults 'play' sport and everybody else works to facilitate sport: making sports gear, building stadiums, organising events etc. No other work is done on W. The whole society has been built to follow the Olympic ideal.

But, of course, there is nothing ideal about W. We learn as the novel progresses that far from being a happy, joyful land, it is – in reality – unhappy, cruel and inhuman. Any society based on winning alone – based on overcoming others – cannot be anything other than vicious and unjust. By the end of the novel we realise that the island is more like a concentration camp than a Utopia with its citizens screaming '*Raus! Raus!*' and '*Schnell! Schnell!*' at the athletes, mirroring Nazi brutality.

In his essay 'Philosophy, ethics and sport' the French philosopher and aesthetician Pierre-Henry Frangne says that Perec is critiquing sport in his novel and showing the dangers of accepting sport's excesses and radicalisation. Sport can only be ethical and virtuous, according to Frangne, 'through the moderation of our approach, through the restrained nature of our relationship with it, through the purpose which we confer on it – since it has none of its own, being just a game, a futile activity, even a derisory one'.

The *agôn* is necessary in sport but competition must be qualified and kept in perspective, otherwise anything in sport is justifiable. *Agôn* can turn to *polemos* (war) if we forget that sport is a fiction, a form of play.

We can never lose sight of the fact that sport is – must be – meaningless, while at the same time being compelling. Sport is, Frangne says,

> at the heart of multiple contradictions (rule or random, freedom or necessity, gratuitousness or usefulness, moderation or immoderation, pretence or reality, body or thought) which force us, not to overcome them and do away with them, but to do quite the opposite: maintain them lucidly and dialectically, injecting into them a fragile balance, the fragility of which is clear.

The Uruguayan journalist, writer and novelist Eduardo Galeano contrasts the joy of the fan with the joylessness of the fanatic – 'upending whatever once passed for his mind', it remains like an aimlessly spinning shipwreck in wild waters. The fanatic is the fan in a madhouse.

Galeano writes about the fanatic's stridency and aggression, his noise and fuss. I recognise this in my behaviour when I see Munster losing to Ulster in rugby. There I am shouting at the referee in the television, my bitterness in full flow, my resentment mounting as the cheering of the Ulster fans in Ravenhill grows. There they are: old sectarianisms and prejudices of which I would never have thought myself capable, spewing out of me.

To the fanatic, the enemy is always in the wrong and is always deserving of a thrashing. The fanatic sees the enemy everywhere, even in the quiet spectator nearby who might have a more balanced opinion – that the referee might not be wrong, that the Ulster fans are entitled to cheer on their team, that the Ulster players might deserve their win, that Munster (on the day) might not have been good enough. And so what if they are: it's just a game, isn't it?

Yeah, right.

It's just a game when England's rugby team are hammering Ireland at Twickenham. Their fans are belting out 'Swing Low, Sweet Chariot'. Their players are having a gala, while the Irish are helpless with ineptitude. Old Irish wounds are festering as the game has turned away from us. The fanatic, Galeano says, has much to avenge and I have, too, against England – the old oppressor, the old enemy. As if a simple game of rugby (a sport I never played) could avenge 800 years of bondage.

But, somehow it does. We Irish celebrate the great football win over England in Stuttgart in 1988 as if it were our greatest sporting achievement. Over thirty years later we sing 'Who put the ball in the English net?' as though it still matters. As though it is some small revenge for the Famine and the Battle of Kinsale.

But, in sport, we fanatics excoriate not just old enemies, but our own. How often do we hear football fans boo their own players off a pitch after an ignominious defeat? I have heard Munster rugby fans bristle when Tomás O'Leary made a mistake in Thomond Park. I have heard Cork hurling fans complain about Timmy McCarthy losing possession against Limerick.

At a game in 2018, when the very young hurler Mark Coleman hit a bad wide, I said something like 'Jesus, Mark, that's terrible.' The man beside me, whom I didn't know, replied, 'He's only a young fellow, he's doing his best.' I resented the comment. I didn't want to be rational or to have my brain rule over my heart. I wanted to be the fanatic and not the fan. Perhaps I had no control over it.

Mark Coleman is a young man who has made sacrifices to be on that pitch. I know these sacrifices. An amateur sportsman, he has trained and dedicated his life to the game. He has pitted himself against others who are older, more experienced and stronger. He has suffered losses and anxieties to be out there wearing that jersey. He was only twenty years of age and had put himself in a position of great vulnerability to be judged by 40,000 people watching on.

And there I was, fifty-seven years of age, passing judgement. I have earned no right to criticise him. I am on a day out, drinking pints and eating fast food with my friends. Chatting and laughing and enjoying myself. Mark's family are watching on in an agony of nerves and hopes and fears. What is my stake compared to theirs? What right do I have to judge him in any manner whatsoever? But I still do it. And when a rational fan beside me points this out – politely and discreetly – I am filled with resentment.

But I'm far from the worst in this behaviour. In November 2021 hundreds of football matches were cancelled in the North Dublin Schoolboys and Schoolgirls League (NDSL), the Metropolitan Girls League (MGL) and the Eastern Women's Football League (EWL), because eighty referees withdrew their services.

The NDSL chief executive Tony Gains said the referees' decision had come about due to inappropriate conduct from managers, players, coaches and supporters.

'This weekend a female referee refereeing her first game of three games was abused so badly from the time she entered the pitch, she decided that she was not taking any more of this abuse from these people and she has now decided to give up refereeing entirely,' he said. 'Another young referee who has only been refereeing for the past two months was petrified on the pitch, he was so afraid even to collect his gear. This abuse he took was absolutely disgraceful.'

The question is why the managers, players, coaches and supporters think it is acceptable to abuse and assault referees. And what this has to do with boys and girls aged seven to eighteen playing football.

Galeano describes the fanatic (me, in a moment of ill-humoured judgement and many others, week-in week-out) in the midst of the crowd as a dangerous centipede. He is a cowed man, cowing others. He is a frightened man, becoming frightening. The fanatic is taking his fears, his losses, all the wrongs of his life and putting them on the shoulders of the young and beautiful sportspeople playing their hearts out on the pitch.

'Here,' the fanatic says to the players on his team, 'take all the wrongs of my life and make them right. And if you can't make them right, it's your fault and not mine. And you – my enemy in that other jersey – it's your fault, too. That I'm frightened, that my life is shit, that my job is shit, that nobody likes me. And as for you, referee, everybody here hates you – you will never be respected or applauded.'

The Cork rugby player Simon Zebo was racially taunted at a rugby match in Belfast by an Ulster fan in January 2018. This, in the genteel world of Irish rugby. This, despite the fact that Zebo is Irish and has played for Ireland with distinction – alongside many Ulster players. And the Ulster fanatic who abused Zebo on that day would have cheered him as he scored tries for Ireland. But it didn't matter – in that moment Zebo is one of the *other*, and he is also of mixed race, so the opportunity for casual racism is taken.

We also know from Lee Chin, Seán Óg Ó hAilpín and others about the racial taunts they have endured on GAA pitches. We know about the homophobic taunts that Dónal Óg Cusack has endured and the abuse that Travellers such as Andy O'Brien of Wicklow have received. Drew Wylie, a member of the Protestant community, has been the victim of sectarian abuse for years, according to teammates in Ballybay, County Monaghan.

When Nathan Breen's family moved to Kerry from Wales in 2006, he took to Gaelic football and began playing with the local Beaufort Under 12 team. But, because of his accent, he stood out. In 2019, on the eve of leading his club to the All-Ireland final he said: 'The amount of grief I got starting out for a long portion of underage was tough stuff. If I had a euro for every time I was called a "fucking Black and Tan" or an "English cunt" – I had to listen to that for a good few years.' This is underage Gaelic football in Ireland: the racial abuse of a child.

So much for male sports fans. How about players? We know about the domestic violence frequently perpetrated by sportsmen – just search 'football player assaults girlfriend' or 'baseball player assaults girlfriend' or 'footballer assaults' and the hits are in the tens of millions, from sports all around the world.

Books by Anna Krien (*Night Games*), and Deb Waterhouse-Watson (*Athletes, Sexual Assault and Trials by Media: Narrative Immunity*) highlight behaviour in Australia, where there have been twenty-seven cases involving fifty-seven footballers and club officials relating to sexual assault and rape. Without one single conviction. Waterhouse-Watson documents how the clubs and the media protect the players through what she calls a 'narrative immunity' against allegations of sexual assault – by invoking old sexist stereotypes against the women, which cast doubt on their claims of being assaulted.

In 2018 this issue came to Ireland, in what is now known as 'the Belfast rugby rape trial', when two international rugby players, Paddy Jackson and Stuart Olding, were tried for the sexual assault of a young woman. Once again, this did not lead to a conviction, but there was public outrage at the WhatsApp messages the players had shared with other men, bragging: 'We are all top shaggers'; 'There was a bit of spit roasting going on last night fellas'; 'It was like a merry-go-around at a carnival'; 'There was a lot of spit'; 'Love Belfast Sluts'; 'Pumped a bird with Jacko on Monday. Roasted her. Then another on Tuesday night.'

What chilled me most were the messages from the victim to a friend on the following morning before she decided to go to the police. 'Worst night ever. So I got raped'; 'They are scum. It's that schoolboy rugby attitude times a million'; 'Thing is I would report it if I knew they would get done. But they won't'; 'And that's just unnecessary stress for me. It's also humiliating'; 'It will be a case of my word against theirs … and because there's more of them they'll all have the same fabricated story about me being some slut who was up for it. It will serve no purpose for me but be embarrassing'; 'I am not going to the police, I'm not going up against Ulster rugby. Yeah, because that'll work.'

The reason these messages are so chilling is because they were so prescient. She knew that the men would be acquitted after a horrible trial where her underwear would be paraded before a public court. She knew she would be accused of being a silly girl who consented to group sex and then regretted it. She knew that going up against Ulster Rugby would be pointless – going up against men's sport would be pointless.

While some rugby players had supported their teammates in the trial, the industry – realising a commercial backlash after the adverse publicity and brand damage was inevitable – disowned the players and cancelled their contracts. This, despite the non-guilty verdict and the players' claims of innocence. Following criticism by the *#IBelieveHer* movement and a protest outside the headquarters of Ulster Rugby, the club and the Irish Rugby Football Union sacked the players. When, in June 2019, London Irish signed Jackson, Diageo withdrew their long-term sponsorship of the club. The decision was inconsistent with the company's 'values', it said. A few months later, when London Irish were due to play in Cork, threats of pickets at the ground forced the club to drop Jackson for the fixture.

It appears that toxic masculinity has become toxic for business, too. Well, well. And if anyone believes this has anything to do with Diageo's 'values', other than valuing its profit, they are deluded.

But should we tar all sportsmen with the same brush? Look at the great things that Marcus Rashford, Sadio Mané and Juan Mata have done for charity, raising millions of euro in good causes. And just because some men who are professional athletes behave appallingly, should we boycott the sports they play? Isn't the culture of sexism embedded in male sport as much to blame as the individual clubs? When I asked one sportswoman if there was sexism in sport, she replied: 'Tadhg, there's sexism everywhere.'

So, is this an issue for society or for sport?

And how are we, as fans, supposed to react? Should supporters of London Irish withdraw their support while Paddy Jackson is playing for the club? And, if Munster were playing London Irish, would I stay away? Or would I walk past picket lines of outraged women, with whom I agree about the Belfast rape trial, to look at a meaningless rugby game?

In April 2019 I was in a pub watching a rugby match between Munster and Saracens when I noticed a Munster fan becoming irate at a comment made by another drinker. Saracens' Billy Vunipola (who had defended a homophobic social media post by Israel Folau) was voted man of the match and the drinker made a joke that it wouldn't have happened if Nigel Owens had been refereeing. Nigel Owens is openly gay. Unlike Israel Folau, who had been fired by Rugby Australia, Vunipola had not been punished. Perhaps he was too valuable to Saracens. Or perhaps liking a Tweet was not such a serious matter to merit sanction.

The Munster fan, who was about sixty, was almost in tears. 'It's not funny,' he said, 'that man is a homophobe. He's a homophobe. My son is a gay rugby player and that man is a homophobe. It's not funny.'

It struck me later that he knew Vunipola would be playing and that Saracens had backed their invaluable player. But he still watched the game, he still took part in it. Yes, he made his protest but wouldn't a stronger protest have been to stay away? Was watching the game not condoning the sport and the Saracens club? However much he wanted Munster to win? And wasn't I condoning homophobia in the sport, by watching the game, too?

In November 2021 Ireland played two international matches within a few days of each other in the Aviva Stadium in Dublin. In football against Portugal, a World Cup qualifier, and in a rugby 'friendly' against New Zealand's famed All Blacks. Both games were keenly anticipated since it would be the first time in twenty-one months, due to Covid-19 restrictions, that the stadium would be full.

In the build-up to the games the sportswriter Malachy Clerkin in *The Irish Times* pointed out that two players, Cristiano Ronaldo of Portugal and Sevu Reece of New Zealand, had serious assault cases against women hanging over them.

A Nevada woman Kathryn Mayorga accused Ronaldo of rape in Las Vegas in 2009, which he denies, but he subsequently paid her a $375,000 confidentiality settlement. In 2019 prosecutors in Las Vegas decided that Ronaldo would not face criminal charges over the allegations and in October 2021 a magistrate judge in Nevada ruled that an attempt by Ms Mayorga to sue Ronaldo for $73 million should be dismissed because her case relied on leaked and stolen documents that the judge claimed were privileged communications between Ronaldo and his lawyers.

In July 2018 Reece had grabbed his girlfriend in a bar and dragged her onto the ground, causing injuries to her face and body. He was tried, pleaded guilty, his girlfriend forgave him and he stopped drinking. He received a small fine for the assault.

In his piece Clerkin says:

> The easiest thing is not to talk about it. To shrug our shoulders and accept that so goes the world. Ronaldo hasn't been convicted of anything, Reece was forgiven

by his girlfriend. So let's just move on and let's settle down to watch a bit of sport, eh?

But of course we should never not talk about it. It's far too important for that. Everyone can make up their own mind on what they see and how they feel. For some of us, any enjoyment of the week is always going to be tempered because these events are hanging there in the background.

Thing is, maybe not talking about it actually is the more honest approach. Maybe it's all a bit weaselly to be wringing our hands and still sitting down to watch. Are we going to boycott either game because Ronaldo and Reece are playing? Of course not. So who's the hypocrite here, really?

Still, Clerkin and some other sportswriters do talk about it and we must continue to talk about it. We have to call it out, otherwise we are failing the many victims of sport's dark passions. We have to call it out so that we never lose sight of what sport should be and what it can be. And what sport should never be.

I 'follow' the Premier League in England. Because I am a Manchester United fan and the club contests that championship annually, I am engaged by the league. I know the clubs, I watch games, I listen out for results. The league is a product and I am an avid consumer. The league has twenty clubs and let's say there are twenty-five players in each club who participate in the first team. That's 500 players. 500 young men. How many of them are gay? Five? Ten? Twenty? Fifty?

That's not the real question, though. The real question is how many of them are openly gay? How many of them are 'out'?

None.

How about the other four leagues? That's 2,500 players. How many of them are openly gay?

None.

How many former Premier League players have come out? Of the tens of thousands of players, many of whom are very wealthy and are no longer dependent on football? One. The German player, Thomas Hitzlsperger.

In 2015 Alan Smith, the former player and manager, said:

> I've had players over the years who were single and read books and so others [other players] said they must be gay ... I think being openly gay would be something very difficult to live with in football ... You can get drunk and beat up your wife and that's quite acceptable, but if someone were to say 'I'm gay,' it's considered awful.

In football, if you read a book it means you're gay. In football, it is quite acceptable to beat up your wife. In football, it is completely unacceptable to be gay. The players are homophobic and the fans are homophobic.

What are the Premier League clubs and the FA doing to end this ongoing blight on their sport? When, in 2005, the FA did try to address the issue, they approached all twenty Premier League managers to become involved in the campaign. All twenty men refused. The FA then approached many players. All refused. Even to be associated with such a campaign was toxic.

As a fan of the league and of football, I am also accepting this ignorance, homophobia, brutality and sexism. It therefore follows that I am part of the problem of homophobia, brutality and sexism in sport.

And it's not just me. The Premier League is the most popular sports league in the world. It is shown live in 212 territories to 643 million homes with a potential TV audience of 4.7 billion people.

Perhaps all of us who engage with sport are somehow tainted by association.

It is the summer of 2019. I'm walking down the Ennis Road in Limerick. Cork have just beaten the All-Ireland champions, Limerick, and I'm feeling good. The Cork fans are buzzing – it doesn't take much for us to roll back out our cocky strut. A lone and drunk young Cork supporter is taunting some Limerick people nearby. He sings (badly): 'We're from Cork and we're better than you, We're from Cork and we're better than you, We're from Cork and we're better than you.' Over and over again he sings it, smiling, pointing his finger at the Limerick fans, walking down the Ennis Road.

Isn't that – at its very core – what sport is? A means for one person or one group of people to say to others, *I'm better than you*? The fact is that if Cork had lost, this young man would not be singing – he would be replaced by a young Limerick man, taunting Cork people. And it's not enough to feel better than the *other* we have beaten in sport, we have to tell them, too. We have to rub their noses in it. We cheer when an opposition player makes a mistake or hits a wide.

We play sport to win. The whole point of playing is to make the *other*, the opponent, lose – to cause them misery. Basically, you do whatever you can to assert your superiority over your opponent and to do that, you must crush them. If you don't crush them, you're not playing properly. If you are very good at sport, you must make others miserable – you have no other choice. It's your job. I've done this many times. Others have done it to me and screamed joyfully in my face when they achieved their primacy over me.

If, as I assert elsewhere in this book, we associate so strongly with the players on the pitch/court/track/ring, that in a way we actually *become* them, then are we not attempting/pretending to be better than ourselves? I become Federer, which means I am a better person than the real me – fitter, younger, richer, taller, braver, better-looking, more determined, more focused, more talented (far more talented). But why do I need that? What's wrong with me as I am? Why can't I be happy being me? Why can't I just admire both Federer and Djokovic and their amazing talents and their stunning beauty, rather than wanting one to beat the other, to assert his primacy – my primacy?

Is being a sports fan, or even a player, just a way to 'big' ourselves up? To give ourselves the appearance that we're better? Is the whole idea of sport just a way for us to judge ourselves as superior to others?

And if so, isn't that a really bad idea? Wouldn't it be better just to live our lives, enjoy our art and our world, have some fun, love our families, love other people (or at least get on with them and not judge them as inferior to what we are)?

Do we really need this? Is this the best we can be? To find ways where we measure ourselves against others? White people are better than Black people. Irish people are better than English people. Manchester United fans are better than Liverpool fans. I am better than the guy marking me. I am from Munster so I'm better than people from Ulster. I'm from Cork so I'm better than you.

There's a story about a western scientist visiting Tibet when the Dalai Lama was a child. The visitor observed a game of volleyball where all the participants wore the same colour uniform and were hitting the ball back and forth over the net without keeping score, and he asked the Dalai Lama what it was. 'Everybody tries to keep the ball in the air,' the Dalai Lama explained. 'When the ball hits the ground it's a sad moment for everyone, and you can see how they all console the person responsible.' The visitor was incredulous and he explained that in his country the whole point of the game was to force the opponents into missing the ball – to *make* the other person sad.

The Dalai Lama was aghast. 'But the ball must hit the ground all the time,' he said, and he began to weep. 'Such a way to play with the human spirit,' he said, and he went to his room to pray.

The moral dilemmas that anybody involved in sport can face – must face – are explored in the seminal book *Loving Sports When They Don't Love You Back: Dilemmas of the Modern Fan* by Jessica Luther and Kavitha A. Davidson.

At the end of the book, in a personal note, Davidson recounts when, courtside, aged fourteen, she first saw Kobe Bryant play basketball in the flesh in Los Angeles. It was a key moment in her life and possibly led to her becoming a lifelong sports fan and a sportswriter. (It is not unlike the moment I saw Con Roche score a goal from a sideline cut when I was ten):

> I can't overstate how much I loved Kobe growing up; I'm a die-hard Knicks fan, but I love watching Kobe play. He was poetry on the court, and I related to him personally as the nerdy kid who was good at math but also loved sports. His persona as an outsider – as the player others didn't relate to, because he spoke Italian and was more of a thinker – really resonated with me.

Not long after Davidson saw Bryant play, he was arrested for sexual assault. She made all the excuses for him at the time and repeated 'every line of victim-blaming'. 'Fourteen-year-old Kavitha made every mistake that thirty-year-old Kavitha calls out from others.'

Now much of Davidson's sports writing centres on domestic violence and sexual assault by players. She herself is a sexual assault survivor. Despite that, when Bryant died in January 2020 she says:

> I was hit with this wave of emotions, just this profound sadness, but also a million thoughts about his complicated legacy … Because, you see, I still love Kobe Bryant; perhaps I never stopped loving him. Every time I see his photo or a highlight of him doing some ridiculous circus move at the rim, I at once feel the

pure joy I had watching him play, profound sadness that he's no longer with us, and guilt over what my continued love for him means for the woman who says he raped her.

Instead of walking away from sport, Luther and Davidson point to the examples of athletes like Megan Rapinoe and Colin Kaepernick who show real heroism and have made real sacrifices to ensure that sport can be better. Instead of walking away from sport, they stand and fight for its soul. As do Luther and Davidson in their writing.

'We have to be better,' Rapinoe said when the victorious US women's football team was feted as world champions in New York City in 2019 and after she stood up to the bully Donald Trump, who doesn't have a sporting bone in his body. 'We have to love more, hate less. We gotta listen more and talk less.'

In the conclusion to their book, Luther and Davidson write:

> There is so far to go [for sport] in so many ways, but at the same time, sports like tennis are diversifying, LGBTQ+ athletes are carving out a space for themselves, athletes from college superstars to WBNA players to professional baseball players are demanding deserving compensations, and owners and mega event organizers are subject to sustained, organized criticism. This is why we can't all just walk away. Sports are worth saving and changing.

MY SPORTS HERO RIKU RISKI

AND SOME QUESTIONS

I N HIS BOOK *HOW SOCCER EXPLAINS THE WORLD*, Franklin Foer travelled around the globe to investigate how football (that most global of sports) could be used as a metaphor for the failure of worldwide economic interdependence to free so many from poverty and corruption.

He writes about how, in the 1980s, English football was used by hooligans as an excuse for violence, leading to a death toll of over a hundred people in that decade. But, while England was the leading producer of football hooligans, violence was also deeply embedded in the culture of football all across Europe, Latin America and Africa.

Martin Alsiö, the Norwegian football historian and writer, has compiled a list of all the football games between 1900 and 2012 where two or more people have died. He can identify eighty such games worldwide with a death toll of almost 4,000 people. The most deadly football game was between El Salvador and Honduras in 1969; it led to a war between the countries and caused 2,100 fatalities. In the eighty games listed, most deaths were caused by the capacity of grounds not being respected, locked exits, bad weather, violence by security forces, accidents and fan violence. Interestingly Alsiö's definition of a hooligan is 'anyone committing violent acts connected to football … actions taken by the legislative powers, those responsible for security at the games as well as all kinds of sub-groups of supporters'. Many of those who died because of football did so because of bad planning and greed. As Alsiö says: 'To the dead it will not matter if they were killed by accident or intention, and we, who are still alive, should focus on accountability rather than our prejudices.'

Foer recounts how in Serbia, Željko Ražnatović, better known as Arkan, used football to turn hooligans, his so-called *Delije* or Tigers, into an army. Arkan said: 'The Delije have left their supporters' props somewhere under the arches of Marakana Stadium and have set off to the war with rifles in their hands.' They sang football songs as they marched. By the end of the Balkan war, Arkan's Tigers had killed over 2,000 people before they returned to football. Many of their victims were massacred in large numbers and buried in mass graves.

In Glasgow, football is used to foment sectarianism and violence with Rangers fans singing 'We're up to our knees in Fenian blood' and Celtic fans singing in praise of IRA sectarian murders. Foer says that both football clubs allow extremist and sectarian sloganeering because they are profiting from it. Glasgow keeps alive its football tribalism, despite the logic of history, because it provides the city with a kind of pornographic pleasure.

Foer documents how football is used by anti-Semites to attack clubs with Jewish backgrounds, such as Tottenham Hotspur, Ajax and MTK Budapest. How Chelsea fans sang: 'Gas a Jew, Jew, Jew, put him in the oven, cook him through.' How West Ham United and Ferencváros fans mimicked the sound of Zyklon gas in the Nazi death camps. How corrupt Brazilian *cartolas* manipulated football to generate huge wealth for themselves and how Pelé was used to give them credibility. How, despite the persistence of corruption in Brazilian football and campaigns to improve ethics in the sport, the national mania for the game has not abated.

Foer writes about the rampant racism in football, the ape noises in England and Italy, the bananas thrown onto the field in Poland, and how such racism was covered up in countries like Ukraine. He writes about the corruption in Italy, how in 1999 AS Roma gave top referees €12,000 Rolex watches and how none of the referees voluntarily returned the 'gifts'. How Juventus and Milan rigged the system of assigning referees to get weak ones who were afraid not to be deferential to such major clubs. And how the prestige and dominance of Juventus did not suffer from such corruption, despite being relegated as a punishment for match-fixing.

So, who is my favourite Italian team? Juventus. Where do I most love to watch matches? Juve's stadium in Torino (now sadly called the Allianz Stadium, after an insurance company). Who is my favourite defender in Europe? Giorgio Chiellini of Juve. Do the ape noises prevent me from watching football? No. Do I love watching Brazil? I do. Do I support Celtic against Rangers? I do. When football hooliganism was at its height and when disasters like Heysel (1985) and Hillsborough (1989) were happening, did my interest in football wane? No, it didn't.

There are new scandals in sport to pile upon the old ones, day on day, week on week, month on month, year on year. Here are a few from my Twitter feed this morning: Gardaí are investigating match-fixing in Limerick; Scott Brown is taunted about his sister, who died from cancer in 2008; Inter Milan fans assure their player Romelu Lukaku that the monkey-chanting by opposing Cagliari fans was not racist; Andrew Luck, who had to retire from the NFL for health reasons, is booed by his own Colt fans as he leaves the field after a pre-season game. All this in one day of sport.

Will there be more scandals and disgrace tomorrow? There will.

Will I continue to ignore them in my fanaticism for sport? I will.

What is Manchester United? It's a business owned by the six children of the late Malcolm Glazer, a US businessman and investor. Why did Glazer purchase this business in 2005 at a cost of €891 million, partly made up of loans secured against the club's assets? Because he knew he would profit by it and in 2021 it was valued at €3.75 billion.

Did I (a United fan since 1968) hate almost everything about Glazer and admire those ethical United fans who fought the takeover and set up an alternative club? I did. Did I do the ethical thing and stop following Manchester United? I didn't. Do I know much about the alternative club, FC United of Manchester? No, I don't.

Is Liverpool FC any different? No. The Fenway Sports Group (FSG) bought Liverpool in 2010 for €424 million to add to their collection of pet franchises. Why did FSG buy this business? For profit and in 2021 it was valued at €3.65 billion.

Despite the bleating of Liverpool fans who adore the socialist credentials of their hero Bill Shankly, have those fans done anything to prevent FSG's shady dealings to depopulate the area around Anfield to 'develop' the stadium?

Did Chelsea fans object to their club being bought by a Russian oligarch, so long as he pumped money into it to buy players and buy subsequent championships? Do other clubs object to ownership by billionaire Arabs or Asians or sponsorship by gambling companies who profit from the misery of addicts? No, they don't, as long as the money piles in and better players are bought. They also buy the fans' loyalty (including mine) – not with money, but with success.

The question is: how much of my moral self am I willing to compromise to see 'my' team win a championship?

The roots of attachment we feel for one team or one athlete over another have to do with a sense of love: a love of place, a love of identity that we learn in childhood. But because there is an us versus them in sport – a struggle – and because we need *us* to overcome *them* (to 'prove' we're better than them), we often vilify or demonise those who represent the *other*. Our love of *us* morphs into our hatred of *them*.

It's one of the reasons George Orwell referred to sport as 'war without the guns'. Orwell hated sport because he was mistreated by sports masters at school who forced him and other boys like him to participate against their will. His experiences led him to regard sport (rugby, in particular) as 'a training ground for elitist bullies who would go on to use their experiences within sport to promote violence and conflict in later life'.

Orwell's famous essay on sport, 'The Sporting Spirit', was in the context of sport being used as a political tool, as demonstrated by Stalin, Hitler and Mussolini; and, more recently, by politicians like Putin, bin Salman Al Saud and the Emir of Qatar – the country which will host the 2022 FIFA World Cup of Football. Qatar wants the world to think better of it, so it's spending hundreds of billions of dollars to make itself look good through sport. This sportswashing reflects the heightened space that sport inhabits in people's estimation – men's, especially.

Qatar also owns the football club Paris Saint-Germain (PSG) through its state-owned share organisation, Qatar Sports Investments. Likewise, the United Arab Emirates (UAE) owns Manchester City via the United Arab Abu Dhabi United Group, an investment vehicle in turn owned by Sheikh Mansour bin Zayed al-Nahyan, the brother of the ruler of the UAE.

In October 2021 the Public Investment Fund of Saudi Arabia purchased an 80 per cent stake in Newcastle United. Qatar (whose state-owned media group beIN holds the rights for broadcasting Premier League matches in the Middle East and North Africa region) had previously objected to the Saudi takeover of Newcastle because beIN had been banned by the Saudi government from broadcasting in its country since 2017. The ban was as a result of Saudi accusations that Qatar was sponsoring terrorism.

Yes, these are the same Saudis who murdered and dismembered journalist Jamal Khashoggi in their Istanbul consulate on 2 October 2018 while his fiancée Hatice Cengiz waited outside. They had gone into the embassy to have legal documents signed so they could be married on the following day. The same Saudis who are currently bombing Yemen into the Middle Ages. The same Saudis who were accused of sportswashing in April 2020 by Amnesty International to cover up a 'sweeping crackdown on human rights, with government critics and human rights defenders arrested, tortured and put on trial, [as well as] a marked increase in executions after unfair trials in the country'.

Once Saudi Arabia lifted its ban on beIN, the Premier League allowed the deal to go through (making more money for ... the Premier League) and thousands of Newcastle United supporters celebrated in the streets. On 23 October 2021 at Selhurst Park, Crystal Palace fans displayed a banner with illustrations of a man dressed in traditional Arabic clothing, carrying a sword with dripping blood, next to Premier League chief executive Richard Masters. A clipboard under the headline 'Premier League Owners Test' showed the checklist: 'Terrorism, beheading, civil rights abuses, murder, censorship and persecution'.

The legal system in Qatar discriminates against women, non-nationals and minorities. In 2016 a Dutch woman was drugged and raped in Doha. When she reported this, she was imprisoned for three months and was found guilty of adultery and alcohol consumption. She was sentenced to one year in prison, but, upon pressure from the Dutch government, the sentence was suspended and she was allowed to leave the country. The man was not tried for rape but was sentenced to 100 lashes for illicit sexual relations.

Amnesty International has long been campaigning for human rights in Qatar. Flogging and stoning to death are legal punishments. Apostasy is punishable by the death penalty. Blasphemy is punishable by up to seven years in prison and proselytising any religion other than Islam can be punished by up to ten years in prison. For homosexuality the penalty for consenting males is up to five years in prison.

According to Human Rights Watch, 'The UAE arbitrarily detains and forcibly disappears individuals who criticize the authorities within the UAE's borders. UAE residents who have spoken about human rights issues are at serious risk of arbitrary detention, imprisonment, and torture. Many are serving long prison terms or have left the country under pressure.'

Does anybody in PSG, Manchester City or Newcastle United – all of which are now state-owned entities – care?

Do any of their fans care?

How many fans of these state-owned entities have spoken out and refused to follow the clubs in these circumstances?

And if Saudi Arabia had bought Manchester United instead of Newcastle United, what would I have done?

It gets worse.

A 2013 report by *The Guardian* highlighted the plight of migrant workers in Qatar. It estimated that construction practices would result in over 4,000 deaths by the time of the 2022 World Cup. The report uncovered forced labour and appalling treatment. Workers were forced to work without pay to prevent them running away. Employers confiscated passports, refused to issue ID cards and denied workers access to free drinking water in the 50°C desert heat. Workers lived in labour camps, up to twelve to a room. Women suffered sexual abuse. This, to build the $45 billion Lusail City from scratch, which will include a 90,000-seater stadium to host the World Cup Final.

When, after an international outcry, exit visas were banned

in 2018 for most migrant workers, about 174,000 people still required their employer's permissions to exit the country. Domestic migrant workers are especially susceptible to trafficking and human rights abuses.

Despite the claims of the Qatari government, *The Guardian*, in October 2019, said that hundreds of migrant workers are still dying of heat stress every year to get the country ready for the World Cup, working in 45°C heat for over ten hours a day. The Qatari authorities are covering up these deaths, attributing them to cardiovascular causes or 'natural death'.

In 1978 I watched the World Cup in Argentina, riveted by the stunning games, the beautiful football and the mesmerising ticker-tape blizzards covering pitches and teams. I remember the splendour of Mario Kempes and the dismay of the Dutch, having lost the final. But I can't remember if I knew about the concentration camps where inmates could hear the cheering from nearby stadiums. I can't remember where I stood on the controversy surrounding the event (I was seventeen) or if I knew that the Argentina government had murdered up to 10,000 people and disappeared up to 15,000 more. I can't remember if I was aware of the campaign to boycott the event in several participating European countries. I only know I watched the event and I loved it.

The question is this: knowing what I know about Qatar and how Qatar is using the World Cup to buy respect and respectability, will I act appropriately in 2022 and boycott and denounce the competition? Will I follow the brave example of Finnish player Riku Riski, who refused to travel to Qatar for a friendly tournament in 2019 due to the 'ethical reasons and values I wanted to act upon'. He did this despite not being a first-team player, thus jeopardising his chances of ever playing for Finland again; let alone in the World Cup Finals. Now that takes real courage and principle – far more than we see displayed on any pitch, track or court. That's real sporting heroism.

Will I stand by my principles and write about the truth? That corrupt FIFA officials took bribes to host the World Cup in Qatar (in July 2020 there were twenty criminal cases pending in Switzerland)? That Qatar must be held to account for its shocking human rights violations? That anybody supporting the competition is putting money in the pockets of corrupt FIFA officials, abetting the killing of migrant workers and supporting the human rights abuse of tens of thousands of Qataris?

Or will I be happy to hide in the sporting collective and put aside my morals and independence of thought? Will I scramble over the bones of the 4,000 people who died so that millionaire players and corrupt officials can make themselves richer? Will my dark, passionate craving for the game (the beautiful game I love) being played by the best players in the world be so strong as to brush my ethics aside?

Another issue, mainly in the United States since 9/11, is the militarisation of sport. Nowadays, US sporting events are often used as a forum for military recruitment and also as a means of paying tribute to the military along with its values and its mission – thus sport is linked with and is used to approve militaristic political aims, and the trillions of dollars being spent on those aims. One sees this mainly at college and professional American football games, but it's also visible at golf and other sports events. Interweaving our love of our team with the political will to pursue war is a very effective means of propaganda, and difficult to counter-argue. The fervid emotions we feel about our sporting heroes at events are passed on to the military 'heroes', making any rational assessment of such wars impossible.

In their 2009 article 'American Football, Flags, and "Fun": The Bell Helicopter Armed Forces Bowl and the Rhetorical Production of Militarism' Michael Butterworth and Stormi Moskal argue that 'through this military-media-sport spectacle, sport effectively is war. It literally brings the military to the sporting public, immersing fans in the machinery of war and enlisting them to rally around the troops.' Thus, real war (causing the deaths of hundreds of thousands of people) is sold to the public as a sanitised (sports-like) version of war and the public passively consumes it as they do games. More recently in the US, authorities have attempted to pass on this emotional transfer to other uniforms such as those of police officers to counter movements such as Black Lives Matter. But one unlikely effect of the 2020 upsurge in support for BLM has been the activation of sportspeople to political action and the forcing of reactionary organisations such as the NFL to accept that it was appropriate for Colin Kaepernick to take the knee during the national anthem as a counter to institutionalised racism in the US.

But why didn't that happen sooner? And will American football now embrace Kaepernick as the great sports hero that he is? Will any of the franchises take him on as a poster boy? Will he present the Vince Lombardi Trophy at the next Super Bowl?

What do *you* think?

There are many other issues which bring shame to sport and those involved in sport: criminal gang participation in boxing; corruption in the organization of football; child abuse in swimming, football and gymnastics; mass cheating in cycling, baseball, athletics, boxing and other sports; the cruelty towards animals in horse racing, showjumping, fox hunting, eventing and greyhound racing – not to mention the savagery of hare coursing.

The continuous spread of gambling addictions through sport and the inextricable links between sport and the gambling industry continue to grow, worldwide, causing mass misery in its wake. As far back as 1999, the National Gambling Impact Study Commission suggested that deregulating gambling on sports in the US could draw $400 billion in bets per annum.

The list goes on.

And by continuing to follow sports and to effectively turn a blind eye to these issues, how culpable are sports fans? Is calling out these issues (as some commentators are doing) enough, or should we begin to cut the ties with sport until it changes? And what if it can't or won't change?

And then there's Rupert Murdoch. Why am I not a fan? Let me count the ways. His destruction of the inherent societal value of a free press. His support of Thatcherite politics and Thatcher herself. Decades of lies and socially destructive vomit spewed out by his evil newspapers like the *News of The World* and *The Sun*. His hatred of the EU (because it stands up to him), his support of Brexit and the damage of Fox News, including the election of Donald Trump. His hostility to gay marriage. His championing of fossil fuels and the ongoing destruction of the planet by climate change, which most of his 'news' outlets deny. His use of football as a battering ram to facilitate pay-per-view TV for the enrichment of the 1%.

So, why then, do I give him my money?

Because of my addiction to sport.

I subscribe to Sky Sports and, while I know that Murdoch no longer owns that organisation, I did give thousands of euro to the bastard so that I could watch sport. Now I'm giving thousands of euro to some other bastard. And I know that one of these evil moguls is as bad as the next but the question arises: who would I not pay, to feed my sports habit?

If I learned that the owner of a sports provider was a paedophile, racist or neo-Nazi, would I stop watching sport?

If I learned of rampant corruption, or widespread homophobia and sexism in a sports organisation, would I stop supporting sport?

If sport facilitates dictators and oppression and horrible moguls, would I stop watching sport?

Or would I turn a blind eye because of the nature of my addiction and the nature of sport – what Jean-Marie Brohm and Marc Perelman call the 'narcotisation of the conscience'? In their book *Le Football, une peste émotionnelle* (*Football, an Emotional Plague*) the authors claim that the institution that is football (in reality all organised sport) promotes corruption, financial speculation, financial wheeling and dealing, cheating, multiformed violence, doping, xenophobia, racism, sexism and complicity with totalitarian regimes and police states.

They speak of the 'opium of sport' and its 'idolatry'. And we cannot cherry-pick which sport we like and don't like or separate the different individual elements of sport. Football (sport) can only be understood in placing it in a global framework of worldwide capitalism of which it is a perfect mirror.

The dark passions the millions feel in sport, they say, are really an infantilising drunkenness or narcosis, a type of fiddling while Rome burns.

Perelman, in his book, *Le Sport Barbare: Critique d'un fléau mondial* (*Barbarian Sport: Critique of a Global Scourge*) states that sport is the world's twenty-first-century new and only true religion. Everybody is flocking to it and everybody is joining in. This is difficult to disprove. I do flock (with all the other sheep) and join in. If you're reading this book you probably do, too.

Perelman sees this global force as possessing an authority that encompasses, hangs over and permeates a society in confusion. In fact, sport is society's only project steamrolling modernity, eliminating all obstacles. Society has no other project, he says, except barbarian sport.

I agree with a lot of what Brohm and Perelman say. But, despite this awareness and this agreement, will I give up my dependence on sport and go into recovery?

Or will I keep my subscription to pay-per-view TV and watch the golf highlights from Wentworth tonight? Tomorrow, will I watch some of the Rugby World Cup? On Saturday will I tune in to the Premier League and on Sunday will I be watching Ireland versus Scotland? Then a GAA match on Sky? Next week there is the Champions League again, will I catch some of that? Man City v PSG should be good.

In October 2019 I went to a book launch in Cork. The writer Caelinn Hogan was launching her book *Republic of Shame*. The book tells the story of how the Catholic Church colluded with the Irish State to conceal, punish and exploit 'fallen' women. In the Magdalene laundries girls and women were imprisoned and used as a form of slave labour. In mother-and-baby homes pregnant women were hidden away and their babies were sold into adoption. And people are still suffering because of these abuses; this isn't a problem of the past.

Hogan's book is brilliant and hugely important.

At the launch, before Caelinn read from the book, a woman told the story of her mother. How she had been put into a mother-and-baby home and how her baby (the storyteller's sister) had died there and was buried in an unmarked grave. (Many babies died needless deaths in these homes due to medical negligence and other Catholic Church priorities.) She spoke of her mother's heartbreak when the nuns who ran the home lied to her about the location of her baby's grave, and how her mother searched but couldn't find any sign of the grave in a graveyard just outside Cork city. A horrifying and scandalous story, painfully told, but how important it is for such stories to be told and to be heard.

When I thought about the importance of this issue and the suffering and despair it caused (is still causing) to thousands of people and their families, I felt embarrassed. When she signed my copy of the book, Caelinn wrote: *Tadhg, thank you so much for listening to these voices.*

Here she was, devoting her life to this vital cause and what am I doing? Writing about sport. Writing about the games people play, the games I played and the games I now participate in as a fan.

There are more important things out there than playing games. Issues like how women are treated in society, issues like direct provision and the overwhelming issue of all – climate change – need to be addressed and discussed.

But, instead, I'm writing this.

Meanwhile, thousands of families still mourn loved ones who died so that football fans can enjoy the 2022 World Cup in Qatar. And while multimillionaire professional golfers try to enrich themselves further in the Saudi Golf League, the dismembered remains of Jamal Khashoggi are still missing. And his fiancée Hatice Cengiz waits for a justice that will never come.

AM I SEXIST?

From the beginning the Greek ideal was an aristocratic one ... Sport was reserved for the best (*ariston*) and the well-born (*eleutherion*), who were also assigned physical and moral virtues (noblemen were expected to be *kalos* and *agathos*, handsome and good). It was practised by men alone, and only free men at that. If Greek sport was *ethikos*, it was only within the restricted framework of this aristocratic ideal, and it served as a means to categorise, distinguish and exclude, reinforcing and safeguarding a social order that was inegalitarian by design.

– 'Ethics and Sport in Europe',
Dominique Bodin *et al.*

*A*MATEUR, A BOOK BY THOMAS PAGE MCBEE – a trans man – tells the story of his training to fight in a charity boxing match in Madison Square Garden. One of the chapters in the book is called 'Am I Sexist?' and he says that the question isn't whether or not he is sexist, but how. He kept a tally of how often he talked over people at work and whom he talked over more often. It was women, at a rate of three to one. He saw all the many subtle ways in which he took men a little more seriously; how he was quicker to respond to their emails and messages, more concerned with their perceptions and more swayed by their arguments.

I don't believe I'm sexist. I have never been accused of sexism by my wife, or female work colleagues or family members. Elizabeth Strout, Kate Atkinson, Zadie Smith, Joan Didion, Deborah Levy, Tana French, Wendy Erskine, Danielle McLoughlin, Sinéad Gleeson and Olivia Laing are among my favourite writers. Mary Oliver, Maya Angelou, Emily Dickinson, Victoria Kennefick and Elizabeth Bishop are among my favourite poets. I can't imagine a world without the music of Joni Mitchell, Sandy Denny or Emmylou Harris.

I look up to my wife and my sisters and my female work colleagues. I never had a problem with reporting to a woman in my job. I deplore the barriers that girls and women have to face in so many aspects of life: in work, in relationships, in the arts. I am appalled at the way women are treated in sport. Yet ironically, when it comes to sport, I think I am sexist.

How, otherwise, can I explain why I don't watch women's sports (on the rare occasions when they are shown on TV)? How can I explain why I don't go to women's games, in particular the games of the Cork camogie team, who are playing my game, for my county – who play it brilliantly – and who have been far more successful than their male counterparts recently?

McBee questioned his attitude to women because of an incident in a gym, when he was sparring against a woman. She was stronger and more aggressive than him and it rankled. He didn't mind being bested by male fighters in the ring, but when she goaded him to hit her and then gave him instructions in another sparring match, he resented it.

In 2006 the Ryder Cup came to Ireland and my golf club, Mallow, had the idea of our own mini-Ryder Cup: the men versus the women in the club. Bad idea. I was selected for the men's team and I foolishly agreed to participate. I was to play a foursomes match with another man against two women.

As I was getting my clubs out of the car before the match, another member, a man, approached me and warned me that we – the men – *had* to win or our existence in the club would not be worth living. He was serious. His wife was on the women's team. He gave my playing partner the same 'pep' talk. I was immediately nervous. This had never occurred to me, but what if my partner and I were beaten and the men's team was beaten by the women? The shame of it. I'm not a great loser (despite plenty of practice) against men, but to lose against women? That would be unconscionable.

Why? The two women we played against were good, competitive and experienced golfers and we were giving them shots and they get to tee off well ahead of us. So what if we lost?

Or was I being sexist?

Sexism is everywhere in sport. In December 2018 a young female Norwegian footballer, Ana Hegerberg, was announced by French DJ Martin Solveig during the award ceremony in Monaco as the first-ever female winner of the Ballon d'Or (the fact women had to wait from 1956 until 2018 for an award says a lot). And at that very moment, the high point of her short but very distinguished career, Solveig thought it acceptable to ask Hegerberg to do a suggestive dance (a twerk) – presumably for the delectation of all the men in the room.

In 2017 Rena Buckley, one of the most decorated GAA players of all time, who has won eighteen All-Ireland medals with Cork camogie and Gaelic football teams, was invited to present medals to Under 12 boys and girls at a West Cork GAA club. At the last moment one of the organisers told her that the club didn't want her to present the medals to the boys after all. He didn't say it, but the implication was that only men could present to boys, only men could be sufficiently heroic or suitable role models for boys.

The roots of organised sport in the nineteenth century are deeply male-centric, as were most other societal institutions at that time. Organised mass-appeal sport was invented by men, for men. Most sports and athletic disciplines were designed by men for men, to glorify 'masculine' attributes like aggression, strength, height, power, endurance and speed. But the rate of change in sport has not kept up with the drive for equality in other areas of society.

While women's sports have grown in both participatory popularity and fandom, they have to fight to eke out every single concession from the patriarchy controlling organised sport. Ireland's greatest current sportsperson is arguably the professional boxer and world champion Katie Taylor, yet it's only since 2012 that women were allowed to compete in this sport in the Olympics, while men have been winning medals for boxing since 1904. And, to do this, Katie and other women had to 'audition' at an event before the International Olympic Committee (IOC). (Even then, only three weight divisions were allowed for women, while men have ten.)

Bizarrely, there *was* a women's boxing event at the 1904 Olympics, but it was only for display – again, for the delectation of men – and not for medals. Equally bizarrely, the IOC initially wanted the women boxers in the 2012 London games to wear skirts instead of shorts in the ring because it would appear more feminine (in boxing!) – until a campaign was put in place (by a woman) to knock that on the head.

Or perhaps it isn't bizarre at all, when one considers the 2004 suggestion by Sepp Blatter, the president of FIFA, on how to increase the popularity of women's football. Blatter suggested the women wear more feminine clothes like they do in volleyball. 'They could, for example, have tighter shorts.'

Blatter has been banned until 2028 and is currently under criminal investigation but other dinosaurs have replaced him. The Norwegian women's beach handball team were fined by the European Handball Association's disciplinary commission for wearing shorts rather than bikini bottoms in the July 2021 Euros tournament. In that sport men could wear tops and shorts 'four inches above the knee', but women were forced to wear midriff tops and bikini bottoms. Thankfully, from January 2022, women can wear 'short tight pants with a close fit' and a 'body fit tank top' when competing, replacing the midriff tops and bikini bottoms.

Despite some progress, sportswomen are still discriminated against and objectified by men. The people least surprised by the twerking question in Monaco were sportswomen – they've been putting up with it for years. And when a lone male tennis player, Andy Murray, criticised the event, his individual stance was remarked upon and lauded, whereas there should have been an avalanche of censure by sportsmen – footballers, especially. But there wasn't.

Some men still seem to think that it's okay for women to appear in boxing rings, but only if they are wearing bikinis and high heels and parading with signs that indicate the number of the next round. And some men also seem to think that the only women who should appear at the Tour de France are those who are pretty and young and whose job it is to kiss the winning riders on the podium after each stage. And some men seem to think that the only women who should appear at NFL games are the cheerleaders in their skimpy costumes jumping around to divert them during breaks in the game.

Then there's the matter of *Sports Illustrated*'s annual swimsuit issue. That a sports magazine deems it fit to even produce such an object in the twenty-first century is remarkable in itself. That it is accepted and consumed by men interested in sport is deplorable, given that it clearly (according to the Australian feminist activist Caitlin Roper): 'contributes to and reinforces the second-class status of women, the notion that women exist for men, for their enjoyment and use, and that women's value is determined by their physical appearance and sexual appeal – essentially, their ability to attract men.'

The Super Bowl is American football's seasonal climax and the largest sporting event in the USA each year. In 2018 it was held in

Minneapolis and a warning was put out for girls in the region in relation to sex trafficking. The Minneapolis police force said it was working with twenty-three law enforcement agencies, patrolling the web to target people buying sex online and monitoring hotels for sex trafficking. With a million fans set to descend on the city, the authorities knew what to expect. According to Forbes.com, 10,000 prostitutes were brought to Miami for the Super Bowl in 2010 and 133 underage arrests for prostitution were made in Dallas during the 2011 Super Bowl.

What is the National Football League (NFL), doing about this, with its status as the largest single entertainment organisation in the world and its annual turnover of $14 billion?

And by consuming the annual Super Bowl (which I usually do) am I not, somehow, condoning or disregarding the frenzy of crass commercialism and sexual exploitation that goes with the event?

One of the reasons that outmoded and sexist masculine thinking is still prevalent in sport is because, unlike in other cultural outlets, sport is still segregated. Women (with a few exceptions, like horse racing, ultramarathons and showjumping) only compete against women and men against men. This would appear strange in music or literature or art (male and female artists do not appear in separate galleries and museums), but it is the norm in sport. And because sport is a competitive form of behaviour and is primarily power-based, men have an obvious advantage.

Women are considered inferior because they are generally physically smaller, less aggressive, and have much lower levels of testosterone. If you don't win, you're a loser and if women can't win against men, then they are losers and can't be given the status of men. Or so the warped thinking goes.

Sport is also different to other art forms in that it is engaged in, primarily, to win, and not to participate. There are competitions in music, art and literature too, but that isn't why those arts exist. However, in sport the contest is everything.

Sport, in some ways, has a multiplicity of shades of grey, but when it comes to winning and losing, it's a strictly binary world. It's men or women, it's win or lose. This is one of the reasons that intersex and transgender athletes are forced to undergo highly invasive scrutiny in order to even compete. In reality, as Erin Stewart points out in her essay 'Tennis, Outer Space & Breastfeeding in Public: the Surprising Relationship between Sports & Feminism':

> this kind of bullshit that women and non-binary athletes face is off-putting and limiting. If a chance of rain can dissuade you from your plans to go to the gym, imagine overcoming complete marginalisation, erasure, abuse, and violence in order to get through the intense, multi-hour training regime that is required of elite athletes. It's hardly mystifying that even highly coordinated women and non-binary people feel alienated from sport – because they are.

In his book *The Toxic Masculinity Crisis*, Denis M. Brown looks at some of the characteristics of this behaviour in men and the first one is ruthlessness. But in fields like business, politics and sport (all dominated by men), ruthlessness is seen as a quality, not as a term of reproach. In sport, taking pity on the opposition or even showing concern during the game for their potential loss would be disastrous and would, in a way, be going against the whole idea of sport.

Another feature of sport is that, by its nature, it is perceived to be of the body alone. I disagree with this perception as simplistic but, unfortunately, it exists. In men's sport, it's of the men's bodies. In women's sport, it's of the women's bodies. And societal tropes about masculinity and femininity are such that these bodies are very often sexualised, for both men and women, but especially for women.

That is a social failing, not only a sporting failing, but it is a fact that athletes are obsessed with their bodies – because their bodies are the primary instrument for achieving success.

Sportsmen objectify their own bodies as types of tools for the team and what can be done with them. Unfortunately, this has led some of them to consider women's bodies in the same way. In their warped world, sexual relations with women become another contest, or battle of wills, where they have to be ruthless and dominant, to win at all costs against what they perceive as weaker opposition.

Because of a sense of entitlement (which sport confers on its highest practitioners, who are looked upon as somewhere between celebrities and demi-gods), and the urge to share 'victories' with their peers, some sportsmen have viewed sexual encounters with women as another type of game to be enjoyed, shared and boasted about, rather than the deeply transgressive and life-destroying assaults that they can be.

This comes from the top down, from the patriarchy all the way through men's sport. In *Volatile Bodies*, Elizabeth Grosz says: 'patriarchal oppression ... justifies itself, at least in part, by connecting women much more closely than men to the body ... At best women's bodies are judged in terms of a "natural inequality,"' which in turn leads to the logical conclusion that women are inferior and therefore should have an inferior role in society – and, one could conclude, an especially inferior role in sport.

Misogyny is rampant in every walk of life. Women can still become world leaders, film stars, award-winning writers, presidents, prime ministers and business gurus – but in sport, because of the physical differences, women often cannot compete with men. And in sport, competing is everything.

Inequity between men and women is not only true in the participation and management of sport but also in how it is reported and covered in the media. Scientific gender studies have actually shown that, in the recent past, the media simply did not have the narrative framework to talk about female athletes in a respectful way. Rather, coverage often actually reinforced traditional stereotypes pertaining to the image of femininity and female sexuality.

One 2017 scientific study of sports coverage in *The Irish Times* showed that over a period of four months, women featured in about 4 per cent of the coverage in the images published. Only one image of a sportswoman for every twenty-four images of men. This is in line with international norms except during events like the Olympics. Despite this disparity having been highlighted for decades, even modern high-quality outlets purporting to support gender equality have not changed.

This is also true of online coverage where it might have been hoped that reporting would be more equitable. One study by

Galen Clavio and Andrea Eagleman of the top ten sports blogs noted that 'males received significantly more photographic coverage in sports blogs than did females, and that female portrayals were far more likely to be sexually suggestive in nature'. Study after study highlight a 'tendency within the media to sexualise, trivialise and/or infantilise sportswomen'.

In 2019 the men's Senior All-Ireland Gaelic football final between Dublin and Kerry was a draw and the replay was scheduled to take place on Saturday 14 September – the day before the women's Senior Final between Dublin and Galway (and two other women's finals). Across four of the Saturday newspapers there was, on average, six times more coverage for the single men's game compared to the three women's games combined. One newspaper had seven times more coverage of horse racing than the biggest day of the year for women's Gaelic football, involving teams from six counties.

Despite the paltry reporting, 56,114 people attended the women's games, making it one of the most popular Irish sporting events of the year. On the Monday after the men's and women's finals the coverage was again badly skewed in favour of the men – except for photographs. The women footballers proved too photogenic to resist.

Sport discriminates against women in so many ways. The Irish women's hockey team brought about a wonderful sense of national pride and togetherness in 2018 by reaching the World Cup Final, but had to pay for some of their own costs in London (something their male counterparts would never have to do). Women's teams like Mourneabbey and Slaughtneil and Milford and Johnstownbridge can bring about a deep sense of community spirit – creating social capital and collective identity, inspiring countless girls who have to face barriers their brothers don't need to worry about – but they get almost no press coverage.

These are the two extremes of sport. The yin and yang. Do I adore one and deplore the other? I do. At the same time – like most men – while following very little women's sport, I have no problem occupying myself with the billionaire fiefdoms of the Premier League, the machismo and greed-fuelled franchises of the NFL and the FIFA men's World Cup, which is saturated by corruption.

Does that make me culpable, by association? I think it does. When I had the opportunity to boycott apartheid South Africa's goods and to support Dunnes Stores workers who refused to handle them, I did it. Why don't I now boycott all newspapers and sports media outlets who discriminate against women athletes? Instead of writing for them, why don't I back away? Or take them on?

While I can and do admire and appreciate great sportswomen, I don't have a strong emotional bond with them or their teams. The roots of my attachment, out of which grew my childhood love of sport, were male players (George Best, Jimmy Barry-Murphy), male sports (football, hurling) and male teams (Manchester United, Cork hurling). Best and Barry-Murphy were the people I aspired to be, they were perfection, the ideal I longed to emulate. When I dreamed of being a player I dreamed of them. When I watched them, I was them. And they are men, not women.

These early attachments are why girls and boys fall in love

with sport, and why they become infused with the impossible desire that is sport – and the impossible perfection it appears to promise. And though I greatly admired Angela Downey and Billie Jean King when I was young, I didn't aspire to be them. I should have, perhaps, but it was an even more binary world in the 1960s when I was growing up. If I had been awarded my Under 12 medal by a great sportswoman like Rena Buckley, maybe my sporting aspirations and interests would have been more inclusive, but I wasn't. The sad thing is that young boys are still being indoctrinated in the same inequalities today.

There is so much to admire in women's sport.

It doesn't have a fraction of the brutality of men's sport – the vicious, casual, arrogant aggression we see all the time in men's football, rugby, hurling, American and Australian Rules football.

It doesn't have the homophobia – in the 2019 Women's World Cup of football, forty-two of the players were openly gay. In men's football nobody can be openly gay – his life would be a misery.

It doesn't have nearly the level of cheating and drug-taking as men. It doesn't have nearly the same level of financial corruption and greed.

I don't believe it has the same level of racism. In reading Azeem Rafiq's account of rampant and institutional racism in the Yorkshire cricket team to a House of Parliament committee in November 2021, I was struck how much of the aggression and racist posturing resulted from a macho and hyper-masculine culture inside the club. Rafiq, who is a Muslim, also described his harrowing first experience of alcohol at the age of fifteen. 'I got pinned down at my local cricket club and had red wine poured down my throat, literally down my throat,' he said. The assault was carried out by a Senior player. Nobody stood up for the boy while it was happening, nobody dared to challenge the brotherhood of toxicity. I can't imagine a Senior women cricket player doing that to a fifteen-year-old girl; nor can I visualise such racism in a women's cricket team.

Women's sport is mainly fuelled by the pure spirit of enjoyment, and of wanting to play and compete and win. The motto of the Olympic games is *citius, altius, fortius*, (faster, higher, stronger) and it represents, according to Pierre de Coubertin (the father of the modern Olympic Games and a sexist to the expansive tips of his moustache) 'a programme of moral beauty'. He said that 'an Olympiad with females would be impractical, uninteresting, unaesthetic and improper'.

Sportswomen are not taken seriously by men. They don't get the proper media coverage they deserve. They have to struggle for sponsorship. They have to overcome bodily issues like periods, pregnancy and breastfeeding – and they do. They play in front of empty stadiums. They train like demons. They suffer the same agonies and enjoy the same ecstasies as men but in so many ways they are treated as lesser than men.

I know, too, that if I had a daughter and she played a sport – any sport – that I would suddenly be very interested in that particular women's game. I would become knowledgeable and engaged and I would attend as many of her games as I possibly could. If she played football or camogie I would probably be a girls' coach. But is that a real interest in women's sport, or attentiveness towards a loved one and her dreams of glory?

There's another issue about women's sport from a male perspective and it has to do with sexual attractiveness.

When I was a child and I idolised George Best and Jimmy Barry-Murphy, I idolised what they did with their bodies. I wanted to do what they did, with my body. So I identified with their bodies and, in a way, I objectified their bodies (and my own) and associated them with great feats of football and hurling.

But I don't identify with women's bodies. Women's bodies are attractive to me, but in a different way, a sexualised way. That doesn't mean that I can't admire a great volley by Caroline Wozniacki as a great volley, but when she posted a picture of herself in a bikini on her holidays recently, I didn't see the body of a tennis player. I saw the body of a sexually attractive young woman in a bikini. And that doesn't mean I can't look behind women's bodies generally, in all the day-to-day activities of everyday life – I can and do, all the time.

I can only look up to Elizabeth Strout, Rebecca Solnit, Mary Morrissy or Zadie Smith. I know I'll never be as good a writer as any of them. But I can identify with them through their prose. I don't believe I have ever considered the sex of a writer when choosing or reading a book. It's their writing that matters, not their gender or anything to do with their bodies. But is this equally true for me in how I perceive female athletes and women's sport? I don't think so.

If my wife saw a picture of, say, Rafa Nadal in Speedos perhaps she would have a similar response to mine looking at Caroline Wozniacki in a bikini. When I look at a picture of him I'm looking at a tennis player who happens to be a man. When Ciara looks at it, she is looking at a sexually attractive man who happens to be a tennis player.

Now, if I were at a tennis match watching Wozniacki play, I would know I'm at a tennis match, watching a game of tennis played by two great women players. In that context I am not sexually objectifying either player, however they look. But is it possible for us to completely disassociate the issue of attractiveness from the body? Especially when the bodies of most athletes conform to notions of attractiveness, fitness, health and youth? With modern sportswear for some sports also revealing much of the body?

Women's sport itself sometimes uses this attractiveness to promote their games.

The Women's Tennis Association (WTA) has published calendars featuring players in glamorous clothes and non-sporting poses. WTA spokesperson Chris De Maria (a man) said in 2002: 'We don't ignore the sexuality part of it. It's part of our marketing for sure because it's a positive part of what we have to offer.'

In 2009 the All England Club admitted that 'physical attractiveness was taken into consideration' when assigning Wimbledon court assignments. Officials assigned the prestigious Centre Court to lower-ranked but conventionally attractive players and relegated higher-ranked but 'less attractive' players to outer courts.

In 2015 Marco Aurelio Cunha, the head of co-ordination for women's football in Brazil, said that growth of popularity of the game was partly down to the sexual appeal of the players. 'Now the women are getting more beautiful,' he said, 'putting on make-up. They go in the field in an elegant manner.'

In 2002 the Ladies Professional Golf Association employed experts to teach women golfers fashion, hairstyles and make-up techniques as part of a five-point plan to attract more fans to the sport. I presume they were targeting women as well as men fans.

It isn't a coincidence that for most of Serena Williams' career she earned less in endorsements than Maria Sharapova, whom she beat in nineteen out the twenty-two times they played each other. As Jessica Luther and Kavitha A. Davidson point out in their book: 'It's no stretch to say that marketers believe their consumers are more interested in worshipping the beauty of tall, skinny white women over and above well-built, muscled Black ones.'

But does the marketing of attractive women athletes really entice women or men to watch women's sport? Or does it merely reinforce the sexual objectification of women's bodies and demean the athletic accomplishments of those women? And does it help to ensure that, in sport – one of the most popular consumer products on earth – women continue to be looked down upon? Black women especially.

Would the sexualisation of female athletes really entice parents to encourage their daughters to engage with sport? Or encourage girls to take up sport? As Mary Jo Kane said, when men look at famous women athletes in the swimwear issue of *Sports Illustrated*, they are not looking at sportspeople at all; they are not watching 'a women's athletic event but sportswomen's bodies as objects of sexual desire'. And when Kane and a colleague at the University of Minnesota carried out a series of focus groups based on gender and age (18–34; 35–55), the findings indicated that a 'sex sells' approach offended the core fan base of women's sports: women and older men. Even young men said that while the sexualised photos were 'hot' they would not encourage them to watch more women's sport.

So, what would make women's sport more attractive to watch? Kane says that the focus should be on great sporting traditions, rivalries, legendary coaches and, most importantly, the showcasing of sportswomen as physically gifted, mentally tough, physically tough, graceful-under-pressure athletes.

Would that be so hard for men to do?

LOSING – THE

ANONYMOUS SUBSOIL

I WAS IN A MINDFULNESS MEDITATION CLASS a few years ago
when a man in his thirties explained to the group how not
being able to play hurling and Gaelic football had led him
to a mental breakdown from which he was still trying to recover.

He outlined how he had never felt the same purpose in anything he did after sport. Even in his marriage or the birth of his
child. Certainly not in his job. He could never replicate the sense
of belonging and joyful fellowship he had with his clubmates and
teammates. The poor man had a hollowed-out look. He looked
closer to fifty than thirty. His eyes were fearful. He moved uncer-
tainly and kept his head low. He was thin and shaky from years
of medication. I was shocked to see him and to hear him tell
his story. It made me think hard about when I stopped playing.

I was still fairly young when I stopped playing competitive football for my club, Mallow United. At twenty-six, I hadn't even reached my peak. Ciara had just finished college and started a job in Limerick and I wanted to spend my winter weekends with her more than I wanted to play football. I certainly don't regret it (Ciara and I have been married for thirty-one years) but it was a pity I stopped playing football – the game I loved so much – when I was so young.

When Mallow United hosted Athlone Town in the 1991 FAI Cup (the biggest game in the club's history), it was a few years after I'd retired. I attended and I was sad not to be playing beside my old teammates. When I met the manager Tommy Conroy after the game he told me I should have been out there on the pitch and I felt a mixture of guilt and loss. I was sorry, too, that my team had lost the same day. It never occurred to me that my presence on the pitch would have made any difference to the result (I wasn't *that* good), but still … there was self-reproach.

On the night after my last hurling match, also in 1991 when I was thirty years old, I cried in a pub in Cork and Ciara had to console me. I cried because we lost and I knew I'd never win a county championship with Mallow, that I had let them down again. I always seemed to let my team down or at least I felt I did.

Maybe I cried because I knew I'd never play championship hurling again.

I had been a hurler since I was sixteen and the idea that I'd never wear a jersey again, never hold a hurley again, never walk out on to a pitch with other men again was a jarring, final and brutal prospect.

I think I moved on from hurling quickly – I was getting married in the following month and my career as a librarian was progressing. I had a lot on. Sure there were moments, when I'd be at a Mallow hurling game and think, *I'd love to be out there*, but they passed quickly and didn't linger. I was asked a few times to come back but I knew it wouldn't have been right for me. It was over and done with.

I certainly didn't feel the acute loss of the man at the mindfulness class, whose life had fallen apart when he could not play anymore.

Nor did I feel David Foster Wallace's sadness when he watched the great tennis players like Roger Federer, his sense of regretting what he could never have been. I love watching the great players – the greater the better, it has nothing to do with me or what I could or could not have been. My dreams of greatness ended in my teens and never returned.

Everybody must stop playing competitively sometime. I knew that too.

Deep down, I think I also knew and accepted that loss is utterly integral to sport. And the final loss is when you can't play anymore.

The fact is that I was never that ambitious about sport. I loved to play and I tried as hard as I could, but that was it. When the Mallow United manager Tony (Tucker) Allen went to Cork City he asked me to go with him – to play at a much higher level – but I said no. I didn't want to play with anyone except my hometown. But had I been ambitious enough, I would have. League of Ireland is the highest level of football in the country and most players would have jumped at the opportunity.

Unfortunately, I was not most players.

When I was picked for a game on the Cork AUL team, I didn't turn up. A teammate told me he would have slept in a tent outside the ground the night before if he were offered a game (even though it was at the end of December), but I wasn't interested. I was also offered a place on the Cork Junior hurling team and I said no. I was also asked to transfer to Senior hurling clubs in Cork city and county and I said no.

I played championship hurling for the Cork Under 21 team in 1981 and we were beaten by Tipperary. The following year I was underage again but I tore my hamstring badly and wasn't fit for the first-round game. The team went on to win the All-Ireland, so they certainly didn't need me.

In late 1989 I was invited by Canon Michael O'Brien to join the Cork Senior hurling panel. When Michael invited you to something you went. So I played a few challenge and tournament games and attended some training sessions. Early in the new year I was diagnosed with pleurisy and I couldn't play for a month or so and was dropped off the panel. I might have been dropped anyway, who knows, it was a bit of a stretch and Michael was trying out a lot of players that winter. But it was a definite end to any hope I might ever have had to play for Cork again. And the Cork Seniors went on to win the All-Ireland, as part of the famous double.

I guess I was disappointed when the team began its league campaign without me. But I wasn't distraught in the way that some people might have been. My loss was proportionate, I got on with my life.

I wonder sometimes if there was a certain amount of fear in me, too. That I didn't really push myself or strive hard enough in case I failed. In case my already fragile ego might be further battered.

This certainly isn't a sob-story, 'I coulda been a contender' tale. I think I did okay in sport and I loved it all. And when it was over, it was over. I had no regrets – apart from not winning a county championship with Mallow.

I never felt masculine or powerful from playing sport. As much as I enjoyed winning or scoring a goal or being praised after a game, I never felt the whole man – that's not the way I'm hardwired.

But there are men who do feel that way. And we hear of athletes all the time who cannot cope with not being a winner any more, not being the object of adulation any more. (Richie Sadlier writes about his difficulties in coping when his football career ended with a hip injury at the very young age of twenty-four.)

This loss is especially true of those who played at such a high level that their identity and their sense of purpose was very closely bound up with playing sport. One study by the BBC in 2018 found that over 50 per cent of ex-professional players had concerns about their mental health and well-being.

One in two ex-players of the 800 who responded to the Professional Players' Federation (PPF) survey felt they no longer had control of their lives within two years of ending their careers. Retired athletes spoke to the BBC of 'losing their identity' when they finished playing sport, and experiencing 'loss', 'regret' and 'devastation'.

I don't believe the end of my playing days traumatised me. I wasn't bitter or jealous of others; and when Cork won the All-Ireland in 1990, I was thrilled.

Perhaps my identity was not as bound up with sport as much as other players – like that of the poor man in the meditation class.

Perhaps I was just that bit too removed from the collective to hurt as much as I could have when I no longer played sport. Perhaps the dreams that some players live out in their play are bigger than my dreams of sport.

I got a huge response to my essay, 'Five Moments in Sport', which was published in *The Stinging Fly* in 2019. The essay talks about my father's kiss and the importance of sport to people, and to me. Several people from the US told me how their unfulfilled sporting dreams have dogged their lives.

Then I was contacted by a psychotherapist, Tony Hegarty. Tony is a hurling and camogie coach and a former hurler. He told me that because of a five-year ban by the Cork County Board in 1970 when he was seventeen, he lost out on the opportunity to win a Harty Cup, a county championship and an All-Ireland Minor medal. But the ban also had a huge impact on his life. 'Something inside of me died when that happened and I froze up inside and stayed that way for years,' he told me. 'The couple of years after the ban are a blur of what I now know to be a sort of depression. I went to college, played on the fresher team under an alias and spent all my spare time in the Western Star, drinking Carling.'

When the ban was lifted in 1973 he began to play again but it was never the same and he moved to Zambia to work as a volunteer in 1975. One week after he went to Africa the chairman of the Cork Senior hurling selectors phoned his brother to ask

Tony to join the panel for the league. Cork went on to win three All-Ireland championships over the next three years:

> Two years later I returned from Zambia for my father's funeral, played for another couple of seasons but at the age of twenty-seven, I walked out of the dressing room in Midleton after losing the East Cork semi-final and I knew it was over. I never played another game. I struggled to explain my decision to quit. My brothers and teammates couldn't understand it but I knew I was unable to go on.

Tony said he often told the story of his ban and his quitting hurling at twenty-seven, but

> as if I was telling it about somebody else. Then in 1989 on a Sunday afternoon while on a psychotherapy training course I was telling the story again. There was something in the way the trainer asked me a question about it and the floodgates opened. I cried like never before. I think I cried for a couple of hours.
>
> After that the rebuilding started. I gave up teaching shortly afterwards and began a career as a psychotherapist which I am still involved in almost thirty years later. I have had the privilege of working with many brave, remarkable people, who have trusted me and shared with me their pain and trauma, their hopes and fears. Through this work, and all the adjacent training, I have achieved a sort of healing. I have been very

lucky to be married all these years to the same, sane wonderful woman and together we have reared three children, all now in their thirties. One of my great joys is having a relationship with my adult children that I never knew was even possible.

I know also that in training teams, to which I have dedicated a huge amount of time, there was always a little bit of me trying to turn back the clock and give myself one more shot at a kind of glory. I did win two county championships as a coach to camogie teams, but my greatest joy is the wonderful relationship I have with almost all the players that I trained. Many of them are now coaching young kids and are generous in thanking me for inspiring them.

As a psychotherapist I have worked with many different client presentations but my favourite will always be the athletes, whether male or female. I love to explore with them the pressures, the anxiety and the self-talk in the hearts and minds of people when they play sport in the public eye. I also love to work to help restore those who were broken by that pressure, to excavate the shame, blame and self-loathing that accrue from those traumatic experiences. Through all of these experiences I am growing towards a sense of peace with my own past. I know I wanted it too much and had to self-sabotage. I know the pressure of healing my father and my family was too much for a seventeen-year-old and I know that was what I was trying to do.

I think the fact that, as young boys and girls, our identities and sense of self are so intrinsically linked to our prowess on the field is both the value and the curse. There's always a price to be paid for wanting something too much.

I found Tony's story very moving and it was brilliantly told. I believe that people being damaged by sport is more common than we might think.

But in the context of this essay and this book, the question must be asked: do we want sport too much? Do we invest too much in our sporting dreams and those of our children? Very often those dreams can't or won't come true and what do we do with them, then?

I have many issues with sports coverage – the day-in, day-out, wall-to-wall reporting on sport. The cult of the winner is a special bugbear of mine. After games it's the winner who gets all the analysis, all the kudos, all the coverage and the photos.

Why is this? In theory, sport is about participation, about competing, but does anybody really believe it?

Who is better and who is braver than a) the player who turns up, togs out and tries her best in the sure and certain knowledge that she will lose? or b) the player who is so far superior to her opponent as to have no fear of humiliation or loss?

How good is the night's sleep before the match, knowing you are destined to win? How relaxed is the dressing room before the game?

The rightness of it all, the beauty of the winner takes all. Its binary meritocratic certainty.

Contrast this with the fraught emotions in the pre-ordained losers' dressing room. The determination to give it a go, to put it up to them, to go out fighting, showing spirit and pride. The knowledge that it won't be enough – but still to go out there and give it everything.

But who do we worship in sport? Who do we celebrate? Who do the media laud and go on and on and on about? What is at the heart of the cult of sport?

The winners.

Joyce Carol Oates says the 'opponent' in boxing is known as the man who loses and is dependable. She contrasts how men are contemptuous of a loser's weakness, but how women are struck by 'admiration, amounting at times to awe … for a man who has exhibited superior courage while losing his fight'.

Isn't that gender-based difference interesting?

Oates writes about the pyramid of winning and losing. There is only one winner at the top but many, many, losers on the way down 'shading out into the anonymous subsoil of humanity'. Carrying on that analogy, the single apex stone (winner) placed on top of the pyramid can only stand there if the myriad of other stones (losers) are beneath, giving it a solid foundation.

In a golf or tennis tournament with 120 players, 119 will lose. That's over 99 per cent of losers to less than 1 per cent of winners. And you still think sport is about winning?

Let's say this is an elite championship – let's say it's Wimbledon. For every player who makes it to Wimbledon (120), another 20 have dreamed of and failed to play on those famous courts. So, in fact, for one winner (there can only be one), there are 2,399 losing players.

That puts the percentage of winners at 0.04 per cent (that's four out of 10,000) and the percentage of losers at 99.96 per cent (9,996 out of 10,000). You are 2,399 times more likely to be a loser than a winner.

For one to win, many, many must lose. Sport is based upon this principle.

But it's not one winner to 2,399 losers, is it? In fact, it's much, much more. The cumulative viewing figures for Wimbledon in 2018, for the BBC and ESPN, was over 55 million (excluding all those viewing online or listening on radio).

Why so many viewers? The reason we watch sport is that we want to feel something. And how we feel that something is by putting ourselves inside the players. One of the characteristics of play, according to the French intellectual Roger Caillois, is that it involves 'imagined realities that may be set against "real life"'. Anything is better than real life, so we turn to sport.

The imagined reality of sport is that we *are* those great players. We *become* Novak Djokovic or Kevin Anderson or Angelique Kerber or Serena Williams.

David Foster Wallace calls Djokovic, Anderson, Kerber and Williams an 'exquisite hybrid of animal and angel that we average unbeautiful watchers have such a hard time seeing in ourselves'. So we pay attention to them and we become them and then we can see the animal and angel in ourselves.

But we know this is a fake, a kind of legerdemain. It's childish and silly – who are we fooling?

We know we are not a Djokovic or a Kerber. They are winners and we are losers. We watch sport to pretend we are not losers, but we know, deep down that we are.

As children, perhaps we dreamed of playing Wimbledon. We dreamed of being great and godlike and beautiful and powerful and wealthy and successful and acclaimed and worshipped. That's why we picked up a tennis racket and went to play – to imagine a different reality. When we played we pretended we were at Wimbledon, we pretended we were champions. I pretended I was George Best.

But we're not children any more, are we? That dream died a long time ago. We lost. We failed.

As adults watching sport we are reminded of these losses too: what we will never do, never achieve, what we can never be. We know the gifts we were denied: we watch them embodied out on the court.

As children watching sport we still may dream of these gifts, but as adults we know that it never happened and our time has run out. It won't ever happen. It's over.

Now, we are all losers.

And the statistics? Well if you take one winner and 55 million losers, then in reality (in the 'real life' of Roger Caillois), statistically, everybody is a loser. One in 55 million is a statistical unreality – it doesn't exist.

Sport is played by losers for losers.

We are all in the anonymous subsoil of humanity.

Speaking of subsoil.

Ever watch players on a team who lose a heartbreaking match? The winners jump, trying to leave orbit, getting as high as they can to be seen, to let the world know. 'Look at me,' they say. 'Look up at me, look at how great I am. I'm better than you, I'm above you.'

But the losers fall to the ground. They are trying to disappear into the subsoil so that nobody can see their shame. They belong in the subsoil, they are unworthy, they are shame incarnate – dirt.

They are also utterly alone.

When teams win, the players come together, to hug and to be together. We win in a group, in the collective. It's a shared joy. We celebrate in the collective and want to be among our own to do it. We celebrate over the years, coming together periodically to remember how great we were.

But when we lose, we lose alone; and we want to be alone.

The losing players stay apart on the pitch and afterwards. The shame is catching, like a disease. You don't want to spread it, or to be near others who are likewise infected.

It's like what Tolstoy said about families in *Anna Karenina*. 'All happy families are alike; each unhappy family is unhappy in its own way.' In fact, each member of each unhappy family is unhappy in their own way.

In losing teams, each player is unhappy in their own way. And it's not for sharing.

When I no longer played hurling and football, I took to golf. Eventually, that was really all I was fit for, physically.

I did play friendly football for years – indoor football mostly

– with work colleagues and friends and it was fun while it lasted. It kept me fit and I could play, I felt at home there.

But in golf there were competitions and matches in my club, Mallow Golf Club. Golf can be quite competitive, there is an intricate ranking system called the handicap and many club golfers will play in one or more competitions per week – which means that this is serious sport.

I didn't mind playing in singles competitions because winning or losing wasn't that critical and if I didn't play well I only let myself down and not any teammates. The stakes weren't that high. I won a few things and my handicap gradually came down as far as six – it was never going to go lower because I didn't practise or play enough. I wasn't good enough.

My favourite golf was always with friends, my brothers Padraig and Dermot, and my brother-in-law Michael, where we'd hit the ball around, have a laugh and enjoy it. A bad shot leads to a shrug and a trudge off to try to find the ball. A few euro might change hands and there would be a bit of slagging, all casual fun. I never played in teams for my club because I didn't really have the stomach for the seriousness of that. I didn't want to let anyone down – more accurately, I didn't want to feel the great shame of letting anyone down again. And I didn't want the stress and anxiety before matches where that could happen.

Then I was asked by the captain of my golf society in CIT, where I worked, to play on a staff inter-varsity team in the annual All-Ireland colleges competition. I agreed – big mistake. This was to be my last experience of team sport as a player (and I don't expect to have another) and it was disastrous.

I was maybe fifty or fifty-one at the time and I still cringe when I think about it, a decade later. I got what's called the yips, but in my particular version it meant that I couldn't putt the ball as far as the hole. This was due to pure anxiety – I lost my nerve. Now, if you don't reach the hole, the ball has no chance of going in. And if you are, say, twenty feet away from the hole (say in two shots) and you leave the ball four feet or five feet short with your first putt, there's a good chance (for me) of a three-putt hole – creating a needless bogey five instead of a par or birdie.

I dread to think how many three putts I had in that golf round in Salthill, each one more excruciating than the last. My poor partner, Paddy Caffrey, had to endure witnessing it. And if I'd performed anyway decently (and well within my compass), our team would have won the championship – we narrowly lost.

The feeling of letting Paddy and the team down was an agony – a word which comes, as I've said, from the Greek *agôn*. The Greeks knew their stuff.

Sport is great, isn't it?

It is when you win, but mostly you lose.

And that was that, for me. Sport takes nerve and grace under pressure and I didn't want pressure any more, I wasn't able for pressure.

It was over.

In his memoir about living in Paris, *Paris to the Moon*, the American writer Adam Gopnik describes the 1998 FIFA Men's World Cup of Football, hosted and won by France. Gopnik is funny about football, about the nil–nil games and the lack of entertainment, compared to NFL or ice hockey back home.

Football, he says, is not meant to be enjoyed, rather it has to be experienced. The World Cup is a 'festival of fate' wherein man accepts the hard circumstances of his life. Failure is certain in life, and nil–nil is its score.

And so, the eventual certainty of defeat liberates us to take real joy in 'any small victory' – that one good shot (or tackle, or pass, or putt).

I agree, but this is true of all sports, including, for example, tennis, where there is a score a minute, or maybe two. Eventually, it doesn't matter how many scores there are in a game: hundreds, or none. Ultimately you win or you lose. Mostly, you lose.

We can take it. We know about losing in our lives, we know about ageing, about our loved ones dying. We are all going to die.

Simon Critchley says: 'The worst thing about being a football fan, especially an England fan, is that horrible, poisonous cocktail of foreknowledge and hope.'

We put our hearts out on our sleeve at the beginning of each game and each new season. We got hammered last year but this year will be different. We got destroyed last week but maybe this week it will be different.

We can't help it – we forget all the losses, the inevitability of loss.

We have to forget, otherwise why bother? If Scunthorpe are away to Liverpool, the fans have to hope – even if only for Gopnik's 'one good shot'. Otherwise, what kind of a way is it to live?

There is a readiness to lose, everybody feels that before every game, even the Liverpool fans at home to Scunthorpe know this, however unlikely it may be.

After Scunthorpe are hammered by Liverpool, the loss is felt and processed and put away in the back of the mind but on the next big day out, say against Manchester City, the hope is dusted off and brought along again.

In this way, we accept loss, we embrace loss, we understand loss. We know that sport is about loss.

It's shit, but it's better than nothing, isn't it?

Simon Barnes says that losing in sport is like 'bad love – putting up with the pain, waiting for the sequel to the last good moment'. Bad love is better than no love, isn't it? But 'like bad love, there comes the point of being worn out, when the reward of the good moment doesn't seem worth all the trouble ...'

That's the way I felt after that golf game in Salthill. If I went back in the game, played again, practised harder, dealt with the yips, the hope would return again and who knows? I might play better, I might do something for the team and be something again.

But it just wasn't worth it for me anymore.

Norman Mailer says that defeat is temporary: 'There is all the temporary insanity of loss. One knows that there is a reality to which one can return, at least the odds are great that it will still be there, but reality does not feel real. It is too unsubstantial. Reality has become a theory introduced into one's head by other people.'

Joyce Carol Oates says the opposite. For her, the victory, the win, is temporary. The moment of loss 'is not an isolated moment, but *the* moment – mystical, universal. The defeat of one man is the triumph of another: but we are apt to read this "triumph" as merely temporary and provisional. Only the defeat is permanent.'

I don't believe that anything is permanent.

Yes, the hope of victory is real in the moment before games – for me in the moment before the three county hurling finals I played in for Mallow and the Under 21 Munster championship match I played in for Cork and that golf match I played in Salthill.

And the despair of losing is real after games.

But new hopes replace the old ones and new losses replace the old ones. I'm hoping that Mallow will win the county championship next year, that Cork will win the All-Ireland, that Manchester United will win the Premier League.

Until they don't, and my teams (and I along with them) lose. I lose and enter that mystical and universal moment that is the basis for sport.

This the circle of sport: hope – loss – hope – loss.

If there's a win thrown in there in the middle ('any small victory'), great, good for me. When that happens I can sense a different temporary insanity.

But that too will be followed by loss, until hope replaces it again.

The cycle continues: hope – loss – hope – loss.

And here I am again.

Hoping.

PART 5

POSSESSION

Below in the half-dark,
A boy is hitting a ball against a wall.
Now he races out along the field,
Dancing with it, whispering to it,
As if it were a child or a dog,
As if no world but this existed,
As if this were the world that will exist.

$\qquad$ – 'Footballer', Pádraig J. Daly

I SHOULD SAY SOMETHING ABOUT MY FOOTBALL – the ball my twelve-year-old self is kicking around my house. I remember it very well. It was plastic but maybe with an infusion of rubber to make it bouncy – just the right shade of bouncy, neither too hard nor too soft. It smelled more plasticky than rubber. Just a normal cheap football, with pentagonal and hexagonal markings painted on its surface to simulate a real leather

ball (which is made from such a design, the stitching together
of twelve pentagonal and twenty hexagonal pieces of leather).
The pentagons were black and the hexagons were white – more
off-white by now and scuffed. The word TEXACO was written
on it in black writing over a red star, which means it was bought
(or more likely given free with fuel) at a petrol station.

My ball had one of those little holes to blow it up but I didn't
have a pump. It was perfectly round, unlike a previous ball that
got too close to the fire and developed an unfortunate bulge.
Its slightly mottled surface gave it a grip except for the narrow indented lines around the hexagons and pentagons, which
were smooth.

Eduardo Galeano says that in Brazil

> no one doubts that the ball is a woman. Brazilians call
> her pudgy – *gorduchinka* – or baby – *menina* – and they
> give her names like Maricotta, Leonor, or Margarita …
> she [the ball] insists on being caressed, kissed, lulled
> to sleep on the chest or the foot. She is proud, vain
> perhaps, and it is easy to understand why: she knows
> all too well that when she rises gracefully she brings
> joy to many a heart, and many a heart is crushed when
> she lands badly.

If you told me that when I was twelve I'd have blushed and
laughed. Or maybe just blushed. I didn't love the ball, or anything
like that, but when I was with it, we had the same purpose. It
was a simple extension of my body.

There are many symbolic interpretations of a ball, notably

as an ancient representation of fertility, and I'm okay with that. The philosopher Steven Connor sees balls as being 'both dead and alive, inanimate objects that are infused with will and life, principles of intention that have been frozen into physical form'. That's exactly what my ball was to me when I was twelve: a principle of intention. And the intention was to play.

Once, years later, playing Senior championship hurling for Mallow, my teammate Liam O'Callaghan passed me the sliotar and as it entered my grasp, I realised it was completely red and wet. Liam had been cut between the thumb and forefinger and was bleeding nicely. I hesitated, in shock, but only for a moment. Then I tossed the wet red ball onto my hurley and went on a solo run down the sideline of the pitch in Buttevant. The colour didn't matter, the blood didn't matter, all that mattered was possession of the ball – the ball that had been infused with life and will.

A great hurling coach, John Whyte, explained something vital to me when I was sixteen. 'When you have the ball,' he said, 'it means that nobody else can have it. Your opponent doesn't have it and he can't score without the ball, he can't do anything. Possession of the ball is everything, so you do everything you can to get it and you do everything you can to keep it.'

Michel Serres describes the ball as being a 'quasi-object', oscillating between subjectivity and objectivity, depending on whether it is at rest on the ground, or being propelled at the feet of a footballer. He is correct: when I was away from the ball it was an object, remote. But when it was at my feet, it was subject to me.

Or was it?

Serres also says that the laws of sport are not written for us, they are written for the ball, they are defined relative to it. And we bend to those laws. In fact: 'The ball isn't there for the body;

the exact contrary is true: the body is the object of the ball; playing is nothing else but making oneself the attribute of the ball as a substance.'

Richard Carew also believed the body was the object of the ball. In his description of a 1602 Cornish hurling match (a sport unrelated to Irish hurling) he writes:

> The ball in this play may bee compared to an infernall spirit: for whosoeuer catcheth it, fareth straighwayes like a madde man, struggling and fighting with those that goe about to holde him: and no sooner is the ball gone from him, but hee resigneth this fury to the next receyuer and himself becommeth peacable as before.

When we are not in possession of the ball (or it is not in possession of us) we are peaceable but we still long for it; we want to be an attribute of it again.

Annie Dillard, a sportswoman to her inky fingertips, writes about her baseball in her memoir *An American Childhood*:

> A baseball weighted your hand just so, and fit it. Its red stitches, its good leather and hardness like skin over bone, seemed to call forth a skill both easy and precise … You could curl your fingers around a baseball and throw it in a straight line. When you hit it with a bat it cracked – and your heart cracked, too, at the sound. It took a grass stain nicely, stayed round, smelled good, and lived lashed in your mitt all winter, hibernating.

When I was a child, I never anthropomorphised my ball, but now, decades later – just like Annie Dillard and Eduardo Galeano – I am inclined to do so. Dillard seems to have a clear picture of where her mitt and baseball were when they hibernated. But I have no picture of my football when I was away from it; when I went off to boarding school and left it behind.

Was it in one of the sheds at the side of the house in the dark, gathering dust? Was it in the extension at the back of our garage where we kept our lawnmower and garden tools and implements? If I left it there, surely I put it somewhere out of the way of sharp edges. Was it outdoors in the rain and wind and frost in the long grass at the back of our house? I can't imagine that.

Was it inside the house, maybe behind the back door? I don't think it would have fit there and Faust might have gone at it. Or was it in one of those packed presses in the hall, behind a vacuum cleaner or the mops and brushes? I can't see it there.

I hope it was in my bedroom, behind the door where my younger brother Padraig and I kept our stuff on two rough, low shelves. Near my bed, beside my old shoes and the clothes I'd outgrown and my tattered copybooks from primary school. On top of an old board game, maybe. And maybe Padraig took it out for a kick around from time to time, on his own or with his friends. I hope he put it back again when he was finished.

I think of my ball on that low shelf in my childhood bedroom. The room is empty and the house is quiet during the day. At night my brother does his homework, then sleeps in his bed near the window in the dark.

I am allowed home from boarding school on one weekend in three and on these Fridays I am reunited with my ball and I resume my solo football game around our house. Until Sunday night when I have to go back along that pitiless road to Fermoy.

Me with my heart cracked; my ball on the low shelf in my bedroom, waiting in the quiet and the dark.

A PLACE BEYOND WORDS

I can't write without a reader. It's precisely like a kiss
– you can't do it alone.

– John Cheever

One

I SEE SO MANY SIMILARITIES BETWEEN my writing and my playing
of sport. In a way, my writing is a substitute for sport and I began
to write not long after I quit competitive sport.

Obviously, they are very different, physically. But in so many
ways, the practice and the rigour are very similar.

There is the initiation, the flicking of a switch. There is the
yearning. The feeling that I should be playing/writing. The feeling
that I should be among others playing/writing. When I was a
child it was easy to be among other players – Mallow had GAA
and football clubs. Many of my friends played football and
hurling and I could play with them on the street or in a local

pitch. When I wanted to become a writer, I signed up for an MA in creative writing in University College Cork. I felt I needed tuition in writing (in the same way that I needed a coach when I was playing) and I needed to be among writers, in a collective of writers. The instinct for both was correct, I felt comfortable being taught about craft, and learning craft from my peers.

There is the communion. I felt at home among my writer classmates in UCC, just as I felt at home among my teammates when I played sport. But there is also the sense of friendship, shared purpose, and all that comes with those.

There is the honing of skills. As a child and a young man I practised hurling and football and I was happy to practise, to develop the necessary skills, to get fit and to be a useful part of the team. I felt I belonged at those training sessions, the sense of purpose and moving towards a goal. Since I became a writer I practise my writing – day in, day out – redrafting, reworking, relearning. And I am happy to practise, I feel I belong at my desk, with a sense of purpose and moving towards a goal.

In *On Boxing*, Joyce Carol Oates says that in sport the public sees only the final stage in a protracted, arduous, gruelling and frequently despairing period of preparation. This is also true of art. The sweet sharp poem that makes its way into the book was a lifetime in the creating and stands tall on the hundreds of rejected poems and the thousands of hours of writing. The essence of sport and art is in that unseen protracted, arduous, gruelling and frequently despairing period of preparation. Very often, for the artist, this preparation is done alone. Likewise for the athlete, in the gym or pounding out the miles, alone on the road.

Then there is the doing. The day-to-day going to the desk, going to the studio, going to the track, going to the pitch, going to the court. The acting out of art's crafts and the self-exposition that must come with it. The failure or success, the getting up and getting on with it. The turning up, time after time.

I never knew as a child or as a young man that playing sport was a means of self-expression, a declaration of who I was and what I wanted and where I belonged. But I knew this in my writing immediately. I knew that in every story, every book, every piece of writing, I was putting myself down on the page. I'm doing it right this moment and I will always do it – whether I am recognisable in the story or not. It is me, even if I am pretending to be somebody else, hiding behind somebody else, in my fiction.

At the Cork World Book Fest in 2019 I asked the novelist Salley Vickers why she writes and why we all read. What was compelling everyone present in the theatre that day towards literature in the first place? In reality, I was not so much asking about her compulsion to write – what I wanted to learn about was my own compulsion. Salley Vickers gave an answer I will never forget. She said, 'We write and we read so as not to feel alone.' And the reason I will never forget her answer is because I have, for a long time, felt the same way.

I also think this is why we engage with sport.

When Olivia Laing interviewed artist and musician David Byrne for her book *Funny Weather: Art in an Emergency*, she asked him what music was for, what its purpose was. And he replied that music connects people. I think this is the purpose of sport, too.

And we want these connections. Connections with our past selves and those who came before us; connections with our friends and neighbours, the ties that bind us as communities; connections with our rivals and those against whom we play and pretend to hate, but secretly love.

But it goes beyond that. We also want, as players, to perform – to act. The young player wants to play, she is drawn to it – compelled to it. Sport calls young people to itself, as a vocation. When we meet that vocation, the rightness of it is almost overwhelming. And moments in our sport will provide us with an intensity of feeling that we rarely get outside it.

The way I played my childhood game at home was unique to me. In fact, the very concept of the game – a game I 'invented' – was unique to me. All players are different. The way each of us plays is distinctive to who we are – just as the way every artist creates her art is unique.

Play, like art, is a means of self-expression. Deep down, every author, painter, dancer, musician, sculptor is expressing themselves and saying who they are, where they come from, what they want, what they think about love, life and the universe. That's what I'm doing in this book.

What about every child who picks up a tennis racket, or kicks a ball, or wants to run? When they are playing these games – especially when they begin competing in public – they too are saying where they are from, who they are, what they desire, what they think about love, life and the universe.

When a child goes down to the local football pitch and plays with her peers she is entering a social contract. She is saying: this is me; this is who I am; this is my mother and father, this is my family. When she represents her club, the child is saying: this is me; this is where I am from; these are my values; this is my community; this is my culture; and this is how I express it all in my unique and precious way, beside my friends.

She is saying: all this has value, it is *my* essence, *my* world, and I assert it. Her play is an affirmation of who she is and of the human spirit itself – just as valid and just as moving an affirmation as that proclaimed by James Joyce in his literature.

But the playing and the taking part in games isn't enough. For the player and the artist there must be more. The player and the artist also have to be seen. If I, as a writer, want to say something, I also want others to hear it. I want people to read my books, to engage with them. Otherwise my writing becomes a hobby, something inward-looking, a conversation with myself and not with the world.

Likewise, the player. If the young boxer wants to express her pride in her community, in its culture and who she is, she also wants others to hear this expression, to know what she is saying. To *listen*. The listener is the fan – the person who goes to games to experience the players expressing themselves.

Sport is a performative art. It happens live, unlike, for example, a painting by Vermeer. And the need to be seen to perform – to perform according to the mysterious will of the audience, as Joyce Carol Oates puts it – is part of the play, too.

When I was a child kicking my ball around my house, I was preparing for a time when I would play in teams publicly. I was honing a craft that I would need when I began to play in front of others.

Players want this. We want to be seen to perform in a game. And the relationship between a player and the person watching, the fan, is mutually dependent. Sport wouldn't happen without fans, theatre wouldn't happen without an audience, music wouldn't happen without listeners, writing wouldn't happen without readers. Kisses, as John Cheever says, wouldn't happen without somebody to kiss.

Two

Adrian Duncan's short story, 'Prosinečki', was first published by *The Stinging Fly* in 2018 and it's one of the great pieces of Irish sports writing. The story takes place during some stolen moments in a football match by an ageing, journeyman professional. The player is looking back on his career and comes to the realisation that his philosophy of football has always been erroneous – he'd been playing based on an illusory ethic of the aesthetic. He also realises that his object of desire – to be recognised as a great former pro sometime in the future in Northern England – will never happen. He has failed and now he has to deal with that loss.

The writer Wendy Erskine picked this story to read for the *Stinging Fly* podcast in 2019 and she did so because she saw the similarities in the story between art and football. How the story, ostensibly about football, is actually about art and how Duncan has merged the two. Erskine and her host, the magazine's editor, Danny Denton, draw out the point that, in writing, it isn't the flashy that elevates the work, but what is pragmatic, what serves the story. And this type of Dionysian or Apollonian opposition or conflict [Erskine's words] is what makes art. Erskine says that these models contrast Edgar Linton and Heathcliff, Charlie Watts and Mick Jagger, Tracey Emin and Cathy Wilkes. Very often what's beautiful in writing is what needs to be cut away. There is no beauty without purpose. And this is also true of sport.

The language in the story is not clichéd or typical of sports writing. It is measured but rich. Sport deserves this. Some examples from 'Prosinečki' (interspersed, not one continuous extract):

> When the player was young, he learned how to live a quiet life as a lesser god ... When he was at his peak he could extend his personality into the opposition's shape who could not dismantle it ... He could cast out nets of influence around the pitch ... There was no limit to his Cartesian aptitude ... His tackling was crystal ... He could imagine the game three vectors ahead ... He pushes the ball beyond frames of possibility.

What Duncan is also doing is showing how articulate and intelligent athletes really are. Not in how they speak, but in how they move. How they can calculate thousands of variables of time and space and act upon them. And how they can do this in milliseconds. The articulation of the intelligence of the football player/narrator in the story – in the mimesis of his language and movement – renders this intelligence as true.

But just because most other athletes cannot articulate like Duncan's nameless player doesn't make them less intelligent. Their real intelligence comes from a place beyond words.

What is most impressive about 'Prosinečki' is that it makes

time malleable just as sport makes time malleable – remember we are in *kairos*, not *chronos*, here. The beauty of the language mirrors the beauty of the play but only in a way that furthers and deepens the story. Just as a beautiful act in football is only beautiful if it works, if it furthers the team's chances, so a simile is of no use without a sentence (the narrator/footballer actually uses this image in the story).

The story is about loss, as sport is about loss. The story is about the aching urge to create perfection, just as movement in sport craves perfection. In art and in sport we are trying to move beyond the known frames of possibility, to reach the stars and see the vastness of the universe, and Duncan achieves that in 'Prosinečki'.

Look at a great player: say, Serena Williams. How did she become a great player? As a child, somehow (probably to do with a parent or sibling or peer) she was initiated into sport. She wanted to play tennis. She wanted it badly. Her motivation may have been to please her father, or to best her sister, or to prove herself to others, or to prove what women could do, but whatever it was, she began to hone skills and to practise and obsess and eat, drink and sleep tennis. She watched great players, she saw the adulation they received. She saw their techniques, their fitness, their dedication. She breathed all this in and she practised and practised and practised – she wanted to succeed. She exalted tennis and brushed aside the sacrifices needed to make tennis happen in her life. Then she began to play in games with others and people began to watch her and this was her object of desire. So she practised harder. She lost games, she exposed herself in public, she got hurt. She heard the casual racism, felt the casual sexism and she ploughed on. She became a great sportsperson – one of the greatest.

Look at a great writer: say, Edna O'Brien. How did she become a great writer? As a child, something (probably to do with a parent or sibling or peer) led to her initiation into literature. She wanted to write. She wanted it badly. Her motivation may have been to please her mother or father, or to emulate someone, or to prove herself to others, or to prove what women could do; but whatever it was, she began to hone skills and to practise and obsess and eat, drink and sleep books. She read the great writers, she saw the adulation they received. She hung around with writers. She saw their techniques, their style, their dedication. She breathed all this in and she practised and practised and practised – she wanted to succeed. She exalted literature and brushed aside the sacrifices needed to make literature happen in her life. Then she began to send out her writing and people began to read it and this was her object of desire. So she practised harder. Her books were rejected, they were banned. She exposed herself in public, she got hurt. She felt the casual sexism and the religious-based misogyny and she ploughed on. She became a great writer – one of the greatest.

The Australian poet Fay Zwicky says that sport and poetry require a balance between freedom of expression and restraint, between movement and constraint. A good poem and a good game can be described as graceful, playful and beautiful. Both involve movement (rhythm, propulsion, forward momentum) and flow. In her essay 'Border Crossings', Zwicky writes about the poet needing muscles, 'emotional, spiritual and psychic muscles that transcend the limits of the self'.

How often do we hear of an athlete being 'poetry in motion'?

In an interview with Zwicky (not long before she died in 2017), the writer and sportswoman Charlotte Guest speaks of the inherent beauty in sport. And this is where we often hear of the 'art' of an Osaka or a Salah, in the sense of the aesthetic, the beauty or grace in their movement. Guest asks the question: 'Are sport and poetry beautiful?' and she says that as abstract concepts, they are. But their main beauty is not so much as objects in their own right but 'rather they possess a beauty that always reaches beyond itself, to something more … an ideal that is beautiful in its perfection.'

Guest describes how the artist and the sportsperson are always striving for what they cannot make perfect, but how in that sense of infinity, creating art and playing sport make us forget our mortality.

In his poem 'Sport', Paul Durcan conflates the intensity of sport and art, the compulsion for both and the essential requirements of rigour for both.

It was my knowing
That you were standing on the sideline
That gave me the necessary motivation –
That will to die
That is as essential to sportsmen as to artists.

The poem is also about the sharing of sport, in this case the sharing of a son with his father and the affirmation the son achieves from that.

I have a fuzzy memory of my brother Dermot winning an All-Ireland hurling medal in September 1971, when I was ten. I watched it on TV at home. My memory is of running out of the house into a nearby housing estate. And Paul Redmond, my friend, was running up towards me. We met about halfway.

We didn't hug or anything. We probably just said 'He did it!' or 'We did it!' or talked about the game. I mostly remember my compulsion to share the moment of ecstasy with somebody else. My body could not contain the emotions I was feeling.

In the same way we want to share the best movie we've ever seen or the best song we've ever heard. In the sharing, the emotion is amplified and vindicated and released.

I have been a reader for many years and I equate that to being a fan at a game. As a reader, I can pass judgement on the writing. I can reject it. When my first book was published, I wrote a blog describing the terror of my exposure. It was like being a fan at a match, comfortable in the crowd; and then climbing over the fence, putting on the team shirt and entering the game. Now I had to perform and all those in the crowd – the hurlers on the ditch – were looking at me, judging me, accepting or rejecting me.

Empathy is at the heart of reading and being a sports fan. As a fan, I am becoming the players on the pitch. I am living vicariously through them. And, when one watches a Kylian Mbappé, this is a beautiful feeling. As a reader, I am also becoming the characters in a book. Through empathy, especially if the writer is very skilful, I feel the character's feelings. When I am reading Sally Rooney's *Conversations with Friends*, I become Frances. I am a vulnerable young woman with an alcoholic father falling in love with a married man, and getting lost in that love.

And I want these feelings because it means I'm alive and I'm not alone. Even if Frances has her heart broken or does something vile, I want this to happen to me. This is why I read in the first place.

Children understand these links more than adults. Or perhaps they are just more open about it. When you sit down to watch a game with a child, she will ask: 'Who are you up for in this game?' What she wants to know is how you will perceive the game. Will you be one set of players or the other set of players? The adult might think she is watching objectively or without any real connection. The child knows that there's no such thing as objectivity in play. You are playing or not. And if you are playing, you want to win.

In her essay 'Ok Son?', Wendy Erskine tells how when she would go to the cinema with her young son he would ask at the beginning of the film, 'Which person are you in this?' At some instinctive or subconscious level I think children know that in order to engage with a story, we have to be one of the characters. Of course we do. In fact, we can be all the characters if it's done well. But there is no point in any story if we're not right in it.

And, of course, who we are in the story determines how the story will turn out for us.

It's the same in sport. A game is a story. When the child asks you who you are up for at the beginning of the game, in fact she is asking who you *are* in the game. We're not spectators, we're *in* the game, we're right in there.

In *Wanderlust*, Rebecca Solnit describes her feelings when she came onto the streets with thousands of others to demonstrate against the 1991 US Gulf War. In those moments of shared belief and the shared expression of that belief, she says, she sensed a rare and magical possibility of a populist communion. In those moments, the 'small pool' of her own identity has been overrun by a great flood, 'bringing its own grand collective desires and resentments, scouring out that pool so thoroughly that one no longer feels fear or sees the reflections of one's self'.

She says that these people, in the right circumstances of idealism or outrage, become heroes. Heroes, she describes as people so motivated by ideals that fear cannot sway them. And in the moments of shared action for what is good, everyone present becomes a hero.

Those who attend games as fans are not heroes. But those inside the white lines have been motivated so strongly that fear cannot sway them. And so they put themselves on display to be judged and to risk failure in public and shaming circumstances. They have dedicated their lives to becoming the hero and, as fans (because we are present within that moment), we are becoming the hero too. Our fear cannot sway us during the game, our failures have no purchase on us, our mistakes are erased in the greatness and glory unfolding during the game.

And that feeling is truly wonderful.

James S. Vass Jr says that when fans go to a game, they do it to experience the phenomenon of 'cheering for self'.

There are two transformations at the game (and he writes in the context of a college basketball game) – although he refers to the game as 'an event', which includes all that happens before, during and after the game. This is a distinction I strongly agree with. So much of sport happens before and after the game – especially its rituals.

The first transformation is that the person going to the event steps into the role of fan. Before the event, the fan might be a housewife, physician, student, judge, policeman – anything. But when they attend the game they are transformed into the fan and only the fan. They become homogeneous.

The second transformation is that the fan becomes the player – the star. 'Players,' writes Vass, 'become a proxy for those that no longer play basketball, cannot or never could. Players become representations for fans that identify with the team of players and who share the credit for success and the agony of defeat.' This transformation then allows them (and this is what fans want most of all) to 'bask in the glory of the chosen team's success'.

Art is about emotion. The whole purpose of music, writing, painting, film-making – all of it – is emotion. It's about feeling something – feeling anything. Henry James said that in the arts 'feeling is meaning'.

Art is not an intellectual exercise, even if one has to use the brain to write the poem or the symphony and one has to use the brain to process them. Once we translate that, it is all distilled down to an intense emotion. We want to be Romeo and Juliet. We want to die for love. We want, like Doctor Faustus, to sell our souls to the devil.

It's the same in sport. We engage with our team or the player we love (an emotion) because we want to feel what they feel.

We want to feel young and fit and beautiful and purposeful. We want to have the skill they have and to know we have that skill. It doesn't matter whether we win or lose (and we want to win for sure, but the risk is worth the emotional investment) as much as whether we feel or we don't. Winning is the best thing, but losing is the second-best thing.

And these feelings are in the body. They are not intellectual, they are physical. We feel with our bodies. With our skin, our eyes, our hair, our heart, our lungs, our mouth. Our mouth goes dry in awe of Van Gogh and in awe of Simone Biles. Our heart beats faster, our skin tightens, our hair stands up, our breath quickens.

When I do a reading at an event I expose myself publicly. I know I could make a mess of it, I could choke or say something awful. I know the audience might hate my work, or feel indifferent to it. I feel sick with nerves beforehand. I question why I put myself through this. If the event were cancelled I'd be delighted. If nobody turned up I'd be delighted. These are the exact same feelings I had before a match. The madness of it all, the sheer arrogance to think that I could play well, that I could win. And then – afterwards – the relief. The utter joy that it's over. The pride, the basking in public recognition, the sense of being accepted and worthy. The sense of being somebody.

There is a great risk-taking in sport. Players are vulnerable. There is every chance in sport that one will lose, that one will fail. I knew this in sport and now I know it in writing. Creating art and playing sport take bravery – not a physical bravery (although some sports do require this), but a bravery of the soul. When I send out a pitch to an agent, magazine, newspaper or publisher, there is every chance that it will be rejected – that I will fail and lose. I usually do. Hope and persistence are necessary in sport and writing. If the despair one feels from rejection is greater than the yearning to be read, to be acknowledged as a writer, then one stops writing. I have friends who did this. They were writers and now they are not. I know friends who gave up sport for the same reason. I gave up playing sport myself. Sport and art are callings, but they are also life choices – one can opt out more easily than one opts in.

You can argue that these failures and this yearning occupy other activities, too, even in our everyday lives, such as our work. But in sport and in art, there is the public exposure, the inviting in the reader or fan to judge the performance. This element, the willingness to risk public humiliation, is different from failing at a job or within a relationship.

Three

In her book *Living, Thinking, Looking*, Siri Hustvedt discusses the similarities between playing and writing. One of the most damning accusations of sport is that it is useless. People like Noam Chomsky, Umberto Eco, Jean-Marie Brohm and Marc Perelman look on sport as a distraction from the important aspects of life. But, as Hustvedt points out: was the work of Emily Dickinson useful? Was the writing of Franz Kafka useful? Both of them, for the most part, did not send out their work and Kafka directed that his be destroyed when he died. Art, ultimately, Hustvedt says, is useless. You cannot sit on a painting, you cannot eat a sculpture or use music as a tool. The only purpose of art is to be looked at, thought about and felt. This is true of sport, too. A game will not feed us or clothe us or shelter us. But, like art, it is alive and we *want* to look at it and think about it and feel it and be transformed by it.

Those who deride sport as a meaningless, physical and often brutal activity (George Orwell) would never point to the meaninglessness of Beethoven's *Symphony No. 5*. Because they are moved by music it is meaningful and because they are not moved by sport is it meaningless. They can see the truth in music and therefore it has significance. But I can see the truth in sport and so it is significant to me.

Hustvedt champions the views of D.W. Winnicott, the English paediatrician and psychoanalyst. Winnicott followed on from Freud's *Tummelplatz* and Strachey's playground theories to talk about 'potential or transitional space'. He theorised that it was only through play that people could feel real. And I see this in sport all the time. One of the reasons people are so addicted to sport and why it is so popular is that it feels more real than real life – what Joyce Carol Oates calls 'ordinary life'.

In sport we feel that we are in a kind of hyperreality. This intermediate area, according to Winnicott, is crowded with illusions generated by play, but the 'potential space' cannot be situated only inside the person. It is outside the individual but it is also not the external 'real' world. The transitional object, he says (in the case of a child this could be a teddy bear or a blanket) is a real object in the world, but also a symbol – it is at once a 'piece of real experience' and a fiction.

The origins of play are deep and bodily, according to Winnicott. They begin in the first relationship between the baby and the mother, in the way that they look at each other, in the mirroring that happens there. Play (sport) is the physical exploration of space and our ability to create an imaginary zone of experience: potential space. Hustvedt says that this is where art lives, but for me it is also where sport lives, where our appreciation of sport becomes rooted inside us and whence our love of sport grows.

While the embedding of play is in early infancy, the embedding of sport is in childhood. So, too, is our art embedded in childhood. Louise Bourgeois said that art is not about art. Art is about life. 'All my work … all my subjects have found their inspiration in my childhood,' a childhood that never lost its mystery or drama. The wonder of George Best's perfection (which I experienced in my childhood) has never lost its mystery and drama for me.

Games are a fiction – they are not real. Sport is often described as a metaphor or an allegory. Games are just games, just playing. They are not real (in the sense that they are meaningless) – and yet they are very real because we imbue them with meaning. This is true of all the arts. A painting is just some bits of coloured paste spread around a canvas. But when Caravaggio does this, it is art – it means everything. A game of football is just twenty-two men or women chasing a bag of air around a field – meaningless. But when your team wins the League of Ireland or the World Cup, it means everything.

It is the truth in Caravaggio that makes it real and engaging. It is the truth in sport that also makes it real and engaging. This engagement, to paraphrase Hustvedt, is 'active and creative' not just intellectually, but 'emotionally, physically, consciously and unconsciously'.

Some see this truth in art, some see it in music, some see it in poetry or drama, and I am lucky enough to be one of those people who see the truth in all of those. I don't think it's mainly snobbery that causes some intellectuals to look down on sport (compared to art); some people just don't see the truth there.

I, along with billions of others, do.

Music, painting, dance, film and literature (all the arts) Hustvedt says, are generated by play. Winnicott says we never give up our fictions for the so-called real world. The direct development he traces from transitional phenomena to playing, to shared playing to cultural experiences, is the exact sporting path I took as a child. I played alone with my football around my house. My ball was my transitional object. But as I grew older, playing alone wasn't enough: I wanted shared playing and cultural experiences.

Johan Huizinga, the Dutch cultural historian, argued that all culture is a form of play. Lev Vygotsky, the Soviet Marxist psychologist, felt that play, a developmental phenomenon, began with the imaginary situation. When a child pretends, she 'operates with alienated meaning in a real situation' – the symbol has shifted. When we play and when we play sport, we are operating in a real situation (a game), but the meaning is alienated. In play – in imagination – there *is* a monster under the bed, a fairy flying outside the window, and the result of the game we are playing has a significance beyond understanding and will transform our lives and render us so joyful that we can barely continue to breathe. And so, my father will kiss me in Kent Station.

As I am kicking my ball around my childhood home, I am also happily lost in Vygotsky's imaginary situation. When I chip the ball into my dog's kennel, I am George Best passing it to Denis Law who buries it. When I bend it around the front corner of the house, I am Rivelino bending the ball around the German wall in the 1970 World Cup. I am in the most real of situations in my childhood home, but the meaning of my game is alienated, thanks to my imagination, which is lit up with magic.

In 1996 scientists discovered that neurons in the premotor cortex of macaque monkeys' brains fired when they performed an action such as grasping. But these neurons also fire when another animal merely observes the same action. These are called mirror neurons. In sport, fans can develop a type of human intersubjectivity. We know we are not the players on the field carrying out acts of wonder and glory, but our mirror neurons still fire, allowing us to *feel* as the players do. Hustvedt refers to this as a type of biological mimesis. Plato knew of this mimesis and applied it to the arts, but it was not proven as a biological fact for another 2,000 years in the macaque monkey.

In a way, there is a dialogue between us and the players in the game and we recognise ourselves in the players, as the baby recognises herself in her mother. This reflection – of a better version of ourselves – is something fans of sport utterly desire and we believe it to be true.

Babies are not born with a sense of self; they only learn it around the age of two, when, as toddlers, they develop the ability to reflect on themselves from the perspective of others. In a way, when we engage with art or sport, we deliberately 'unlearn' this skill and give up our own sense of selves to experience the thrill of having the sense of being somebody else.

When teaching young students how writing and reading works, I talk about a plot device from the Harry Potter books, called Polyjuice Potion: the character who takes it assumes the form of another person. But they have to have something from the body of the other person (a hair, for example) to make the potion work. In writing, the magic is more powerful, I argue, because one doesn't just assume the form of another; one *becomes* the other. Because the writer has used something so specific to the character (her essence), we can cross over into the book, and become that person. So, at the end of *Foster* by Claire Keegan, the writing is so perfect that we *become* the nameless child as she runs to embrace the aunt and uncle who have shown her a love she had never known before. As she runs down the road towards the gate where they have stopped, the reader is utterly transformed into that child. We run, too.

This transformation takes place during games. When I watched Séamus Callanan score a goal in an All-Ireland hurling semi-final in 2019, I was so inside the game and the moment and the hurling, that for a second I became that great hurler – it was just for a moment, but I was completely him. I had to steady myself by holding onto the bar counter, so enraptured I had become at scoring such a goal in such a game. The transformation into Séamus was so vivid as to be truly jarring and so was the transformation back into myself afterwards in the sunshine outside the bar. The person who takes Polyjuice Potion feels strange when returning to themselves. I feel strange when I return to myself having been in a great book or a great film or a great game.

Joyce Carol Oates compares watching the great fights between Joe Louis and Billy Conn, Joe Frazier and Muhammad Ali, Marvin Hagler and Thomas Hearns to enjoying a perfectly executed rendition of Bach's *Well-Tempered Clavier*. The fight's mystery, she says, is that so much happens so swiftly and with such heart-stopping subtlety that you cannot absorb it except to know that 'something profound is happening and it is happening in a place beyond words'.

But just because a match is a story without words, it doesn't mean that it has no text or no language, or that it is 'brute', 'primitive' or 'inarticulate'. Rather, the text is improvised in action, Oates says; and the language between the fighters is a dialogue 'of the most refined sort' in a joint response to 'the mysterious will of the audience which is always that the fight be a worthy one'. Only by being worthy can the match overcome the crude paraphernalia of the setting (ring, lights, ropes, stained canvas, sweat, blood, the smell of beer, the blood-lusting roar of the crowd, the slap of a glove on a face, the thud when a boxer collapses on the floor) with its transcendent action. Only by being worthy will the artifice fully work.

The difficulty for those not initiated into sport is that they cannot see beyond the setting or hear beyond what they judge as the brute inarticulacy of the action that is taking place. For them it is like reading dialogue in a language they don't know. I have friends in sport who would never dream of reading a novel, or listening to music. They would say, 'I'm not into reading or music.' The language of music to them is inarticulate. They don't see the truth in fiction.

For me, the lack of words in sport is not a drawback. There are many types of language and communication and there are no words in much of the music of Max Richter, Ennio Morricone or Miles Davis. But it does occur to me that in writing about sport that I am a translator or interpreter of sorts. What I'm articulating is not my own, I'm taking the art and trying to find the right words to describe it. I'm okay with that. It's an honourable role and if I can do it correctly, I will bring the unwritten profundity of sport back from a place beyond words, to a place where we all can hear its story. My astonishment is your astonishment, to paraphrase Annie Dillard.

Another difficulty for some people is the lack of a script in sport. The absence of the master creative artist who has written something wonderful. Oates says that while a match is a story, it is always a wayward story, one in which anything can happen. There is no libretto, no text. In sport the text is writing itself as it goes and it may be a grand drama or not. To the sportsperson, this is actually one of the great attractions of sport. Nobody knows what will happen next.

Dermot Bolger, who wrote two plays about identity that hinged around fans of the Irish football team (*In High Germany*, 1990 and *The Parting Glass*, 2010), says that one of the things fans love so much about sport is that it is not a previously devised text. In effect, the players and the fans are composing the work as they go along. Nobody knows the ending – it has not been written yet. It is, as Oates says, being improvised in action.

This is a thrilling idea. That all the 84,000 people present at an All-Ireland hurling final and the million people watching on TV are creating the story of the game as it happens – the ultimate performative act. Of course those inside the white lines are the main playwrights, but everybody has a role. Second by second, the tension and drama build to an ending that nobody knows. We watch, not knowing but also loving the not knowing. The players, Oates says, are like shadow-selves of each other, but they are also shadow-selves of everyone watching – the million or more people in the game. Aristotle defined tragedy as something 'serious, complete and of a certain magnitude' and this is what we get in sport, too.

It matters who wins, of course it does. But what matters more is that the game or book or film or song is worthy and when that happens, it's more than enough for us.

It's more than enough in sport and more than enough in art.

PART 6

HURT 1: MASCULINITY

WHEN I WAS TWENTY-FOUR I GOT hurt during a hurling match in Kilworth. It was in the second half and I was caught in possession between two Midleton players and one of them nailed me in the back with the heel of his hurley. I remember the moment of the blow and going down, injured, winded and sick.

Feeling sick is not common during a hurling match. Pain, anger, elation, dejection, exhaustion, frustration, sorrow and joy are common, but nausea was not something I'd known before. Nausea might be something you'd feel after a time away from the game, at the first training session back when the coach would push you hard to demonstrate how unfit you were. You'd see the odd fellow retching or puking then, but almost never during matches. Or if someone had a feed of pints the night before a Sunday morning football game, he might get sick after exerting himself – I've seen that, but I've never done it.

Lying curled up on the ground in Kilworth that day I wondered if I would be able to get up and play on. There was only one way to find out. I tried to control my breathing but that wasn't happening. Eventually, I did get up and I readied myself to take the free. I was disoriented and I must have hesitated or looked unsure because there was a shout from the crowd: 'Over the bar, Tadhgie!' I recognised the distinctive voice of Joe Hayes. Joe had often trained Mallow down the years and he was a big influence on my hurling when I was young. His three sons, Gerry, Pat and Jodie, were probably on the team with me that day.

I took the free and I think I scored, but we lost the match.

In the dressing room afterwards I was feeble and not sure what I was doing. My cousin Eamonn Coakley said, 'That fellow is going to faint if we're not careful.' I got a shock when I heard that and I sat down, alone and fearful.

▲▲▲

Chess is not a sport. Card games are not sport, not even poker, which they show on TV sports channels. Chess and cards are wonderful games and have many of the attributes of sport: the initiation, the longing, the years of disciplined solitary preparation, the *agôn* or contest and the opponent (the *other* needed in sport). As in sport, the stakes can be high and life-changing, but chess and cards are not sport.

Sport is a test of physical abilities – it is of and by the body. Yes, behind the physical there is a deep intelligence and a vision forged in childhood and a rigour and a lifetime's crafting of skill and grace under pressure. And there is the will to succeed, to practise, to get up time and again after falling. But in sport the intelligence, vision, will, rigour and craft are channelled through the body. You play sport with your body. You don't play chess or cards with your body; somebody can select a card for you if you cannot do it yourself; you can direct the move in an electronic chess board with your voice.

Andrew Edgar says that Philippe Petit's 1974 act of walking across a high wire between the Twin Towers in New York City was both a form of art and a type of sport. He says that 'sport and art may both be interpreted as a way of reflecting upon metaphysical and normative issues, albeit in media that are alien to philosophy's conceptual language'. Sport's media are muscle, sinew, lungs, blood and bone – very alien to philosophy's conceptual language. Timeless, metaphysical and reflective grace in sport is achieved by the body of an Annika Sörenstam rather than by the paint of a Hockney, the ink of a Brontë, the voice of a Simone or the thinking of a Heidegger.

Not all physical activities, pastimes or games constitute sport. Frédéric Gros opens his book *A Philosophy of Walking* with the line, 'Walking is not a sport.' Walking, Gros says, is child's play; it's just putting one foot in front of the other without the restrictions of time or rules. Sport is all about techniques, time and rules, scores and competition. It is about the cultivation of endurance, and a taste for physical effort and discipline.

Unlike walking, sport is an ethic and a labour. This is true of chess and poker too, but, in sport, the techniques and rules and scores and discipline control *bodily* movements and interactions. Some of them control the amount and type of violence players are allowed to apply to the bodies of opponents. Most sports, for example, (except combat sports) do not permit contact with the head or neck areas, for obvious reasons. Or striking somebody in the back with the sharp end of an ash stick.

According to Steven Connor, there can be no sport without bodily motion and 'that motion must be ... purposive, aimed at a goal'. This is one of the things which distinguishes the movement of sport from that of dance, he says.

Where sport and dance do meet is in the primacy of the body. Nadia Bailey, a former ballerina, writes:

> The dancer's body is not just the tool with which she creates her art. Her body *is her art* and is to be judged accordingly ... Ballet: all freedom, all grace, all illusion, built on a conceit that I can't help but be seduced by, the impossible promise of perfection. But physical, too, all body and sweat. How it must negotiate between those two points: that we are all only bodies, only ordinary, everyday things, elevated by our training, our fierce attention to our art, our deep and lovely surrender.

Again, this is true of sport. On the one hand we are only bodies, ordinary things, but on the other hand we can, through our deep and lovely surrender to sport, negotiate ourselves toward the impossible promise of perfection.

▲▲▲

I was never afraid of physical pain when I played football or hurling. I don't believe I shirked making a tackle or getting stuck in. I wasn't big or very aggressive as a player and I would rarely foul or hurt other players. But in football, when I was a winger, I would go around a full back and if you did that there was always the possibility of getting the legs taken from under you, or worse, but it never deterred me. In hurling I'd put my hand up and if I caught a ball I might take my man on – I was fast. Going towards goal past a man with a big stick in his hand isn't always the wisest course of action – but I wasn't fearful of giving it a go.

I always admired players like Joe Deane and Johan Cruyff because they were willing to accept the physical consequences of taking a ball past somebody. Hitting somebody isn't brave or tough, but being willing to take the hit does require courage and inner strength – as well as commitment. The word 'willing' is based upon the word 'will'. Accepting a blow to your body takes 'will'. Taking one for the team became a cliché for a good reason.

The fear of being branded a coward, or 'yellow', was a far greater threat to me than physical pain and if you got a belt you got a belt and you'd get over it. In the main, I'd been lucky with injuries – I never had bones broken playing sport, for example. But when I was sitting on that long wooden bench in Kilworth, as my teammates showered and changed around me, I knew I was in trouble, and some deep mammalian survival instinct compelled me to seek help.

I walked out of our dressing room and into the Midleton dressing room. This is a no-no unless you're looking for a fight and I was never the fighting type. Dr Dave Boylan was administering to the Midleton team and I knew Dave from boarding school. I got some funny looks from the Midleton players but nobody said anything. I told Dave the story and he said to go straight to hospital but not to Mallow hospital. 'Go to the Regional

Hospital in Cork,' he said. This troubled me – Mallow was a small local hospital, but the Regional was a major trauma centre. Dave didn't elaborate, but he said to be sure to tell them where in my body I was hit.

Derry Mannix – who was our team coach that year – kindly drove me to the hospital in Cork. I vomited a few miles outside Kilworth, but thankfully out the window of the car.

A&E was not very busy – it was a Sunday afternoon. I remember seeing a few other walking wounded in jerseys arrive in – one had an impressive facial wound and a blood-stained white jersey, the other had what looked like a broken hand. I'm not sure if I was in my clothes or hurling gear but I think I was in my clothes and I felt a fraud without a spectacular wound or fracture. I got hit in my back was all I could say, I felt sick and then I got sick in the car on the way to the hospital. I don't feel great or I think something is wrong are pathetic things to say in A&E – how vague and wishy-washy can you be? So the nurses didn't prioritise me, and I didn't blame them.

I was feeling sorry for myself. We had lost, we were out of the championship, and I had not done everything I should have for the team (I was never able to do as much as I felt I should). The usual dose of self-recrimination after losing was fortified by an added guilt at being the centre of any attention or fuss – it wasn't manly, for starters. The whole thing was probably nothing. I got hit, so what? I was sure I'd be sent home any minute with the inference not to be wasting busy people's time with childish perceptions of 'injury'.

▲▲▲

In *Foul Play: What's Wrong with Sport,* Joe Humphries points out that sport 'exacts a heavy toll on public finances through injuries and related lost work hours'. One 1995 study showed that 33 per cent of all injuries in the UK were caused by sport, with football alone costing £1 billion per annum through medical expenses and production losses. That was a lot of money in 1995. An estimated 750,000 people per annum report to hospital A&E units in the UK because of sport.

Humphries says that while children should be encouraged to engage in rough and tumble to learn endurance and dexterity and risk-assessment skills, sport – with its propensity for dangerous excess – is not the place for them to develop. The key question he posits is not *what* health benefits sport provides, but what health benefits sport provides over vacuuming or collecting garden leaves – both of which offer moderate, useful and safe types of exercise, rarely requiring hospitalisation.

A 2017 study of contact sports in the USA by Ray Fair and Christopher Champa estimated the cost of injuries per year as ranging from $446 million to $1.5 billion in college; for high school the range was $5.4 billion to $19.2 billion. These are only the short-term costs; the long-term costs may be much higher. This is *every* year.

The authors also wondered if American football, football, wrestling, lacrosse and basketball should be made non-contact sports. They estimate that this would prevent 49,600 fewer injuries per year in US colleges, including 6,900 fewer concussions; high school sports would see an estimated 601,900 fewer injuries, including 161,400 fewer concussions per annum. That's a lot of teenage concussion.

The authors do not say how wrestling would function, nor

how meaningless the other sports would be without contact – of some kind. Nor does Humphries say whether or not we could codify vacuuming or leaf collection into a safe sport, perhaps to Olympic standard or to have World Cups of their own.

My facetiousness aside, by 2022, thankfully, there is much more concern about issues like the links between concussion, traumatic brain injuries (TBIs) and Chronic Traumatic Encephalopathy (CTE) – a neurodegenerative disease. These are now being studied in relation to sports like American football, ice hockey and rugby. New rules and protocols are being put into place such as the Head Injury Assessment (HIA) protocol in rugby. All sports and their long-term physical impacts on health must be talked about openly and acted upon, especially in relation to children.

Dave Mirra, an American BMX rider and rallycross racer took his own life in 2016. He was posthumously diagnosed with CTE. According to ESPN, in addition to the 'countless' concussions he suffered during his career, his skull was fractured when he was hit by a car at the age of nineteen, and he had also boxed as an amateur in his youth. By 2013 around 4,500 former American football players were suing the NFL to mitigate the long-term effects of concussions. In 2018 the NHL (National Hockey League) settled a lawsuit by 318 former players. These cases and the discussions about the effects of concussion in sport (including the damage caused by heading the ball in football) are only the beginning.

Luckily I never suffered a concussion as a player. I did witness some terrible injuries. In a fractious football game against Ballincollig I saw a teammate's leg being broken. The bone's crack sounded around the Town Park in Mallow and it was revolting. What made it worse was that the Ballincollig player fully intended to cause serious harm. I was sure of that – he dived in two-footed, high over the ball, out of control, studs first.

I don't enjoy people getting hurt during sport – I especially didn't enjoy it when it was my turn. I don't take pleasure in bad collisions or late tackles, but I'm okay with the possibility of them, however contradictory that may sound. Sport is teeming with such contradictions. We have to come to terms with them if we want to maintain our fandom.

I'm all for making sports safer with suitable equipment and rule changes to protect players. But to remove all contact from sport would be to destroy many sports and I can't agree to that. Football without the possibility of a tackle wouldn't be football.

Did I wish that hurling was a non-contact sport when I sat there in the hospital A&E department all those years ago? I don't believe I did.

▲▲▲

There was a change of shift in A&E and a new set of nurses came on and one of them asked me for a urine sample. I went into a small toilet and urinated into a plastic receptacle and it hurt, and my urine was bright red and I showed it to the nurse. 'Oh,' she said. 'You better come through.'

Things started to happen. They put me in a bed and a doctor saw me and he felt around the area where I had received the blow. The next thing I knew I was being prepared for a laparoscopy. The doctor explained it to me: 'We are going to make an incision in your abdomen and put in a scope and examine your kidney to see if it is viable.'

'Viable?' I said.

'It will depend on the damage and the level of internal bleeding,' he replied. He was very matter-of-fact about it. 'There may be other issues too that we don't know about yet.'

When he said that I regressed to a small child and I knew that my fate was out of my control. I had lost agency over my future and what would happen to me. I had been doing something dangerous, it seemed, and I had never previously considered sport – hurling or football or Gaelic football – dangerous. Why had nobody told me that? I'd been playing sport for as long as I could remember. Sport was fun and games, an inherent part of life, what you did or watched in your spare time. It wasn't meant to cause life-changing injuries or lead to the removal of organs from your body.

I settled in to await my fate. I didn't have a general anaesthetic during the procedure and I could see the long stiff tube enter my body. Then I felt a different and sharper pain deep within my abdomen – it was a *wrong* pain. When I saw the scope begin to disappear inside me, I closed my eyes. The doctor told me to stay still and so I did.

After the laparoscopy my sister Cathy came into the room and her eyes were full of love and concern. I was glad to see her and now I didn't feel so helpless or alone in the maw of an implacable machine. I think she held my hand and I asked her to tell our mother and father that I was fine, that everything would be fine. 'Tell them not to worry,' I said. 'I'm going to be fine.'

But in the quiet of that room, when Cathy had gone home, as I was waiting for the results of the laparoscopy, if you had asked me the same question I asked earlier – would I wish that hurling was a non-contact sport – perhaps my answer would have been different.

In that room I was afraid.

The news came soon afterwards that there was no internal bleeding and I wouldn't require further surgery. I would get to keep my kidney – for now.

▲▲▲

I don't like comparing sports – especially ranking them as in: 'this sport is better than that sport because A, B, C …' Sport, like every other facet of life, is full of snobbery, but I've never bought into it. Even with hurling – especially with hurling, maybe, because of its elitist leanings.

However, a distinction should be made between sports that are dangerous and those that are not. Sports that I don't consider dangerous are those like running, swimming, tennis and volleyball – these are sometimes called non-contact sports but it isn't that simple. Gymnastics, for example, is categorised as a non-contact sport, but some of its disciplines (an interesting word) are quite dangerous – contact with a cross beam or the floor from a height can be a lot more hazardous than contact with somebody's hand. The Soviet gymnast Elena Mukhina, for example, was forced to return early from a broken leg against her wishes in 1980 and subsequently fell in practice, breaking her spine and leaving her quadriplegic. She died with complications from her injuries in 2006, aged forty-six.

Likewise, 'non-contact' sports such as equestrian eventing,

ski jumping, skateboarding and cycling are all packed with peril.

Obviously, boxing, rugby, American football, hurling and so on are dangerous sports – the hazards here are in the contact with opponents (or teammates) and their equipment (such as the butt of a hurley).

Does the danger increase our enjoyment of sport? I think it does. The concept of physical courage, of facing down danger, is an attractive one for those who perhaps find themselves personally lacking in this type of bravery. In sport we observe idealised, perfected versions of ourselves – an aspiration. Very few people aspire to cowardice. But is it really cowardice to be afraid of being hurt or hurting others? Or is it sensible? Is that word 'cowardice', in fact, loaded with macho intent and a certain type of patriarchal programming? Likewise being 'manly' and my fear of being branded 'yellow'?

Personally, I'm thrilled at the idea of two football players diving into each other at full pelt, feet first for a loose ball, or two rugby full backs racing headlong towards each other to contest an up-and-under. The possibility of serious injury raises the stakes and makes the moment heftier, more critical and hence more enthralling. And you can hear this in the tone of the crowd during games – the sound reaches a sharp timbre of anticipation in the moment before the coming together of bodies. After a brutal impact there's a great empathic inhalation and groan from those watching. There can be outrage, too. I don't remember if any specific sound was made by onlookers when I fell to the ground in Kilworth that day, but I expect there was.

The stakes involved in a game – the difference between a World Cup Final or a friendly international – further the level of enjoyment and engagement for fans. How much a game matters, matters. Andrew Edgar says that 'the possibility of loss and failure … is inherent to sport' and he is correct, but the scale of the loss is also significant. If the risk involved is the possibility of a career-threatening injury and the end of all the player's hopes and dreams, never to play again – then this renders the game and the watching of the game more meaningful. These risks and losses can occur, as I found out when I was twenty-four.

Yes, any sport can lead to injury and the training can be especially tough on the body, but the risk of injury from a 130kg man landing on your neck is much higher in American football or rugby than it is in badminton. And if Philippe Petit put the rope he walked upon at three feet instead of 1,362 ft above the New York City pavements, would Andrew Edgar have considered his act as either art or sport? I don't think he would.

▲▲▲

When I settled into the renal ward after my laparoscopy I mostly enjoyed my time there. I was relieved to be on the mend. The nurses were kind and I was well looked after. There were some great characters in the ward and I got a good store of yarns out of them. I wasn't in much pain if I didn't move suddenly, but my stomach had gone into shutdown so I could not eat or drink and I was on a drip for ten days. My mother and father and my family and friends visited and I relished the wounded hero role I had constructed for myself. Ned O'Keefe, a kind man and one of my team's selectors, came to visit and I was gratified by the shock on his face when he saw the state of me, on a drip and as white as the linen on my bed. I knew he'd pass on to the town how shook I was, what I'd endured for the club, and I wanted that acknowledgement. I felt I deserved it.

There was one unpleasant moment, a few days after admission. A porter arrived with a trolley to take me out of the ward.

'Where are you taking me?' I asked and a nurse said I was going for a scan to see if my kidney was working.

'I thought my kidney was fine,' I said. 'The laparoscopy showed that.'

'Well,' she said, 'there's no internal bleeding but we have to check if it's working so they will put a liquid into you and scan it to see if the kidney is doing its job.'

'And if it isn't?' I asked.

'Oh, I'm sure it'll be fine,' she replied, as I was being wheeled away.

I had a reaction to the intravenous solution they tubed me into for the scan – it turned out I was allergic to iodine. That was unpleasant, it felt like a heart attack or a fit. I think it *was* a fit. My body started spasming and I lost consciousness, but not before being scared out of my wits. They pumped some adrenaline into me and that calmed things down but it didn't solve the problem of checking out the kidney. So I was sent to the ultrasound clinic where I queued up with the pregnant women for a scan. That sounds funnier now than it was then. I was pathetic with nerves.

My turn came and my gown was lifted off. Jelly was smeared around my side and back and a flat metal scope was moved across my skin. I didn't look at the images on the screen. I wasn't optimistic – pessimism is my default state – about my chances of keeping my kidney and the consequences of that: never again to play sport of any kind. Never again seems a very long time when you are twenty-four and sport is one of the few things you have to keep you tethered to the world. I waited for a telling silence or a sympathetic tone from the doctor, but it didn't come.

The news was good. My kidney was functioning, and I could keep it.

And I would, after all, play hurling and football again.

▲▲▲

When asked how she can enjoy so brutal a sport as boxing, Joyce Carol Oates says that it's too complex to answer, that she doesn't 'enjoy' boxing in the usual sense of the word, that boxing isn't invariably 'brutal'.

Oates also calls boxing a 'celebration of the lost religion of masculinity and all the more trenchant for being lost'. But I never felt masculine playing sport. It was just sport and I was a player. It was what I did, no different from nor more masculine than reading books or watching films or having a pint with my friends. And I know that whether I was boxing or playing tennis I'd feel the same.

I'm sure other men I played with or against did conflate hurling or football with masculinity. That player who broke my teammate's leg probably thought himself a real tough guy, a man's man. But I don't think I felt anything different from what a woman playing sport might feel, despite what some people say about the 'otherness' of women playing sport – especially contact sports. I just took football and hurling for granted, which, in hindsight, I regret.

All I knew was the rightness of it, how good I felt on the pitch with a ball at my feet and my teammates around me and the goal up ahead and a pass to be made and to run on to the return and to take back the ball as an extension of myself. Maybe to take a shot or make another pass or go past a defender. It was never about being a man or masculine or – as some writers call it – hyper-masculine.

It was a game and at the age of twenty-four, I thought it would go on for as long as I wanted – forever, maybe.

But with a ball at your accommodating feet you're only in that moment, there's nothing at all except now. Maybe that's why I loved playing so much. When you're playing, really playing properly, what you're doing is timeless.

▲▲▲

One day my consultant came into the ward and listened to my abdomen. 'Interesting,' he said and he bade his little retinue of wannabe consultants to also listen. Which they did, and one of them was a beautiful young blonde woman. When I saw Rosamund Pike in *Love in a Cold Climate* several years later I was immediately reminded of that doctor in the hospital. I paid special attention to her as she fingered her hair behind her ear and pressed her stethoscope against my flat stomach.

'Well? What did you hear?' the consultant asked them and one of them chanced his arm and said something. 'You heard nothing. Nothing!' the consultant said and rattled off some medical terms I didn't understand, apart from the word 'shock'. He insisted they all listen again to learn what nothing sounded like.

I watched Rosamund again and wondered what it would be like to have a life with her. Truth is, I was lonely those days – I didn't have a girlfriend and I would have loved one but I didn't know how to go about getting one. How wonderful it would have been to have a girlfriend worrying and fussing over me in the hospital. Gentle kisses and a soft hand on my cheek – all wounded heroes should have that, shouldn't they? And pale beautiful Rosamund would have been brilliant at it – I just know she would.

▲▲▲

My favourite sporting injury was when I was playing in a hurling league match for UCC in Limerick in the early 1980s – those heady pre-helmet days. I put up my hand for a ball and somebody pulled across the top of my forehead and I went down in a welter of astonishment and blood.

Nicky English ran over and said: 'Who did it Tadhg, what number? I'll fucking kill him.' I always loved Nicky for that. The best bit was that they had to bandage up my head before I went back on and I felt I must have had the look of a wounded Vietnam War soldier with my bandana-like bandage. When we stopped for food on the way back to Cork after the game I made a point to go into the toilet to see what I looked like, and it was extremely rewarding.

Yes, there was the bandana-like bandage – very dramatic – but even better was that dried blood could be seen through it, and some had leaked down the side of my cheek and onto my ear and neck. I didn't wash it off. When I gave my order nonchalantly to the young waitress and her eyes widened at the sight of me I was delighted with myself.

That night my poor mother had to drive me to the hospital in Mallow to get my cut stitched up. The nurse on duty gave out stink about how dangerous hurling was, while (very roughly, I thought) cleaning around the wound and shaving away some hair to put the stitches in. I must have been wincing and she told me she had an eight-year-old girl in that morning who made less of a song and dance about getting a few stitches.

I put on my best thousand-yard stare – without a single flinch – as she stuck the syringe needle with the anti-tetanus into my arm and then repeatedly plunged her sewing needle through my scalp. I showed her what tough was. Damn right I did. Eight-year-old girl, indeed.

▲▲▲

Sport being a physical activity is one of the reasons it is more popular with men than women, both as fans and players. Eimear Ryan (a writer and camogie player) said in her essay 'The Fear of Winning':

> In a culture where women are most valued for how pretty and agreeable they are, to be given a platform to test female physical strength and courage feels, at times, almost transgressive. Women leathering into each other, striving to best each other, doesn't fit with our notions of femininity. Is this part of why women's team sports don't have the audience that men's do?

Many studies have shown that girls stop playing sport because they feel self-conscious about their bodies, of being judged or laughed at. Ironically, those girls who do continue to play sport are more satisfied with how their bodies look and function – sport having transformed the body from object to subject.

It isn't that boys aren't vain – they are. Or that girls aren't physically strong or competitive or brave – they are. It's what boys and girls *want* to do with their bodies, what statements of self-expression they want to make with them, especially in their teenage years, that determine their relationships with sport.

Rebecca Slater writes:

> The more I pushed myself and excelled in sports, the more I felt I was defying traditional ideas of objectification and femininity. I saw myself as apart from those 'other girls', 'pretty girls', girls who cared about make-up and clothes. I was a strong, powerful sporting woman, whose feelings of empowerment and validation relied on those very patriarchal structures and values I thought I was challenging. This would turn out to be one of my first lessons in feminism, though not in the way I thought.

Sport is about asserting identity and about the ideal – what is achievable by our better selves. Whether that brings a sense of feminism or masculinity or neither depends on the player.

In the earlier military 'Vietnam War wounded hero' comparison I am leaning towards the masculine. These images abound in sport and in *String Theory* David Foster Wallace bemoans this fact. That men talk about their 'love' of sport while using the symbolism of war. 'War's codes are safer for us than love's,' he says. Unfortunately, sports writing and sports talk is rife with the symbols, codes and terminology of combat.

I think the reason we use warlike symbolism is because there is a 'them versus us' element in sport and the ultimate 'them versus us' is war – heightening and clarifying the contest to the limit. But the perceived masculinity of war and those who fight wars is also an element of such recurring symbolism and imagery.

The brave wounded soldier (everyone likes a man in uniform) is, of course, an image to which I clasped when it was made available to me and why I was drawn to that analogy. And the conflation of that with a romantic or sexual attraction is another sporting trope (hence Rosamund and the 'impressed' young waitress).

In playing hurling, as I said, I didn't feel masculine, but when I got that head wound in Limerick and the blood seeped through my bandage I did feel manly, heroic and brave. Perhaps the nurse who attended me that night sensed it and cut me down to size with her eight-year-old girl comment. Which, of course, I had coming, because it was true.

▲▲▲

Twelve days after my kidney injury, my stomach ended its silence in Cork Regional Hospital and I was able to eat again. I was eventually discharged. Although I was living and working in Cork city at the time, I went back to Mallow to recuperate with my parents. My father drove me and the journey was tough, every bump and bend on the road sending stabs through me.

I was thinner and more vulnerable than usual in the following days. Which may explain why, one afternoon, as I was reading in the living room, my mother came in and told me ardently never to forget that I was a Corbett (her family name) and that I was handsome.

I nearly fell off the chair with shock. This was so unlike my mother – an understated and restrained person, not given to such emotional declarations at all (much more my father's style). Perhaps my suddenly prominent cheekbones reminded her of somebody in her family – and I must admit they did suit me. I'm sure the handsome comment was to boost my confidence, which my mother knew was not a strength of mine. I'd say at this time she worried (she was a worrier, one of her many legacies to me) that I would never find a woman to love and who would love me. And I'd given her a terrible scare – when she got word of me being in hospital after a game, in danger of losing one of my kidneys, she must have been at her wits' end.

When my mother said to me not to forget I was a Corbett, I think she was referring to something else, too. I think this was her way of telling me to be resilient, to find my inner steel. To win – not so much in sport as in life. As I said, she was a quiet and understated person, but underneath the gentle exterior there was a formidable resolve, especially when it came to her children. When I played well and won championships, my mother would have said well done and encouraged me, with a modest pride. But whatever tenacity I did manage to aggregate in sport, I knew that much of it was down to her and her people. I think she knew this too.

In July 2017, on the twentieth anniversary of my mother's death, my family gathered at Doneraile Park and then we had a lunch in her memory in a nearby hotel. We told stories and read old letters from her and some new ones to her. I read a poem that I wrote for the occasion and it doesn't surprise me that, in it, I mentioned the best day of my life – my wedding day – and how happy my mother was for me that day. But it does strike me as amazing that I also chose to include in it the moment she told me I was a Corbett and that I was handsome.

Of all the moments in the thirty-six years I had with her, during which I knew her unconditional love and had loved her unconditionally, I chose then: a moment when my mother had stepped outside herself for me. A moment granted to me because I'd been hurt while playing sport.

HURT 2: FALLIBILITY

THERE ARE MANY REASONS WHY ONE individual becomes an artist or a sportsperson and another does not. Very often it's a blurry combination of opportunity, inclination and ability.

Opportunity is key. If Mozart were born the son of a serf in Salzburg instead of the son of a composer and music teacher, would we ever have heard his *Miserere in A Minor*? If Lionel Messi's father did not have the health insurance to pay for his tiny son's growth hormones when he was ten, would we have ever witnessed his genius on the pitch?

Inclination comes from environment and aspiration. Mozart watched and heard his father play music from when he was a baby. Messi's family were football mad, his cousins and older brothers were players and his grandmother brought him to all his training sessions. Of course Mozart would aspire to write music and Messi to play football. And, of course, if Wolfgang Amadeus had a twin brother who was more inclined to fight and become a soldier, he would not have become a composer – he would have become a soldier and gone to war. To excel as an artist or sportsperson you have to really want it, you have to be willing to face down all the obstacles and setbacks and failures and to plough on.

Mozart and Messi both obviously had the ability to perform, too. Mozart had the intelligence, imagination, ears and fingers; Messi has the imagination, intelligence, pace, balance and skill.

In both their cases, their bodies were perfect for their chosen art.

Messi also has courage. He was very small when he began to play. He got kicked by bigger boys but he didn't care. The fear of being hurt – the fear that might prevent others equally or even more talented than him from playing – wasn't a deterrent for him. I think that a lot of people have no interest in sport because of their relationships with their bodies, with how they feel about their bodies and how they react to hurt. Whatever the sport, the body has primacy.

And, whatever the sport, the player must be willing to suffer. Or rather the player *chooses* to suffer, especially in combat or endurance sports. The boxer, Joyce Carol Oates says, prefers physical pain in the ring to the absence of pain that is ideally the condition of ordinary life. Or perhaps, for some people, the physical pain in sport masks, or makes their everyday suffering more bearable.

This could be the physical suffering of the ultra-runner or cyclist. The nervous suffering of the curling player or synchronised swimmer. The disciplinary suffering of putting the craft ahead of relationships or pleasure. The fasting of the boxer and jockey.

The suffering of defeat, too. The suffering of the fear of exposing yourself, of losing, of humiliation, of failure, of hurt. The suffering when you can no longer play.

If you cannot overcome these fears and this suffering you will not want to compete. Your desire to play must be greater than they are, it must inure you to them. But, for some people, the fears and the impact of the suffering will be too strong and they will not play sport.

And most people will accept this and move on – maybe with a greater appreciation of sport and sportspeople. They become fans at an early age and are moved by the spectacles and tension and beauty of sport. Others will dislike sport, and they will turn away.

Which is fine.

A life without sport is just fine. I have many friends and family members who live such lives and they are happy, fulfilled people.

A life without art is just fine, too. I have many friends who live such lives and they are happy, fulfilled people.

Then there are those whose bodies fail them. If Messi had grown up in a basketball mad home, his lack of height may have precluded him from achieving the world dominance he managed in football. He could still have played basketball, but he would never have been a Messi. Many people accept their physical failings and play sport anyway – I did.

If someone has a physical challenge – say, blindness – this precludes them from being a great hurler or footballer. They can still play games, but they cannot compete at the very top levels of sports where hand-eye co-ordination is required, no matter how much they want to do so.

Or if they get an injury – say they break a leg so badly that they cannot run quickly. This means they cannot be a top-class sprinter. Even if they had been a great sprinter beforehand, it doesn't matter. But if they have the urge, they might become a long-distance runner – if the desire is strong enough they will find a way to play sport.

When I was six years old I came across a sack of lime in a neighbour's garden. I threw the lime into the air, it fell into my eyes and I was blinded. I couldn't see for a day or two, but my sight did return (despite having a permanent scratch on my retina). Had I been blinded for life, that would have been it for me as a hurler or footballer.

So, in my case, I did have the body to play sport. I was not big but you don't have to be big to be a great hurler or footballer. Many of the greatest footballers, such as Best, Maradona and Messi are not big men.

My eyesight was okay, despite the lime – even if I did have to get contact lenses when I was eighteen.

I was fairly strong and fast and I had good co-ordination. I wasn't afraid of getting hurt.

But, most of all, I had the opportunity and the inclination to play sport. And I had my dreams.

Shane McGowan's *A Rainy Night in Soho* has the most wonderful line, binding the song with its genius. The narrator says to the woman: 'You're the measure of my dreams.' But for children who love sport it's almost impossible to measure their dreams. Their dreams are embodied in their heroes who contain endless potential, endless value, endless heroism, endless glory.

Their dreams *are* the bodies of their heroes.

Perfect bodies, in the perfect time and place.

Sometimes I wonder, when reading about people like Richie Sadlier or in talking to Tony Hegarty, how different my life might have been if I had lost a kidney and been cut off from sport at twenty-four. That injury – apart from giving me a scare and leading to a moment of intimacy with my mother – didn't have a major impact on my life.

When I got fit again, later that autumn, I went back to playing football with my club. The following spring I went back to hurling. I might have minded myself more at the beginning, but I don't remember consciously doing so.

Around that time, however, I did begin to develop recurring hamstring injuries. I'd tweak a hamstring during a summer championship hurling game. Then I'd have to rest it in the build-up to the next game. This meant that I would not be able to train and I wouldn't be sharp enough during the next match. As a result I might not play well and I might also have to rest my leg after that game.

It was a miserable enough existence: not being in control of my own body, being impotent to the frailty, being imprisoned inside my recurring injury. Not being able to do the things on the pitch that I did when I was younger. I went to physiotherapist after physiotherapist. I did rehab after rehab. I rested. I did all the stretches, applied all the ice, wore a strap, I did everything I was told. But no good.

This was a major contributing factor to ending my hurling days when I was thirty. My body had enough. It was fallible, it had failed me. I was finished as a hurler.

There were other significant injuries, too. The body is fragile.

When I was sixteen, in the very summer when I won my first

All-Ireland medal, I was working in the dairy in Mallow, where fresh milk was bottled and sold. This was the time of glass bottles – pre-Tetra Pak and plastic. The machine to wash the returned bottles was old and chaotic. And sometimes bottles got stuck in the mechanism and had to be freed.

I pulled one such bottle free and it shattered and a long, jagged edge of glass shot sideways into the heel of my right hand. I still have the scar. It meant no more hurling for me that summer but it also permanently damaged my hand. I never felt I had the same touch and strength in my right-hand grip again. I used to wonder, when I was younger, if it meant I was never the hurler I could have been.

But such frailties are common among sportspeople. They will tell you 'I used to play rugby, then I did my knee in' or 'I used to be a runner but my back gave out.' Or a great player 'had a brother who was better but hurt his neck when he was seventeen and never played again'.

Injury and the fallibility of the body are ever present in sport.

In the summer of 2014 I was fit. I'd begun training and cycling the previous year and I'd lost weight and really taken to the bike. In June I cycled a sportive in the Pyrenees with my friend Peter O'Sullivan and was feeling very pleased with myself. At the age of fifty-three I never expected to be in such great shape and, while I wasn't ambitious or fit enough to become a serious cyclist or to compete in races, I was in a good place mentally and physically.

On an early morning ride in July, I crashed outside Carrigaline. I misjudged a turn and ended up hitting a ditch at over 30 kmph and after colliding with the ditch, my body hit the road and I broke my collarbone and a few ribs. Only for my helmet, which was split down the middle like a ripe fruit, I could have been in real trouble. As it was, I was ferried by ambulance to Cork University Hospital and I was a bit of a mess for a few weeks.

This injury did have a lasting impact.

It forced me to think of my mortality and what I was doing with my life.

My job, which had been fairly okay before the injury, began to feel intolerable. My collarbone didn't heal and I had to have surgery in January 2015. This meant a second bout of recovery and a second extended period outside my job. I began writing a novel at that time.

I had always wanted to write and the crash made me think about the end of my time, or at least how limited my time might be – how it was drawing in. I was forced to ask myself (via Mary Oliver) what I was doing with my one wild and precious life.

I also read Helen MacDonald's magnificent evocation of grief and healing, *H is for Hawk*. It contains a sentence that impaled me: 'We carry the lives we've imagined as we carry the lives we have, and sometimes a reckoning comes of all of the lives we have lost.'

I took early retirement from my job and signed up for an MA in creative writing in UCC. I began to learn the craft of writing and to seriously write.

Now, six years later, I have just completed my fifth book.

I'm not sure if I would have had the impetus to begin writing seriously if I had not hurt myself when cycling. My life was changed by that injury. Many lives are changed by injuries in sport.

Sometimes sportspeople don't get a second chance.

In 2019 a rally driver in County Donegal, Manus Kelly, died in a rally. His car smashed into a field after hitting a bump on the road and his injuries were fatal.

He was forty-one years old, married with five children.

He was an excellent rally driver and had won many races. But did he know there was always the possibility of him losing his life while pursuing his sport? Of course he did. All motorsports people do. Was he aware of the many other rally drivers and other motorsports heroes who had died before him? Of course he was.

And, despite all this, he still felt it was worth his while to participate in his sport, to compete against others, to enjoy the thrill of participation, the joy of winning. All motorsports people feel this.

In sports as varied as showjumping, skateboarding, cycling, rugby, boxing and sailing, competitors know that they could, conceivably die while training or competing. But still they do it.

The fragility of the body doesn't matter as much to them as the joy of sport.

The body is fallible – it will let you down. Sooner or later it will betray you.

Ultimately, if injury or death don't prevent you from playing, age will. You will fail. You will lose. You will no longer play.

But still it's worth it.

MY CORONAVIRUS COMEBACK

I WROTE MUCH OF THE FIRST DRAFT of this book in 2019 – it took the bones of that whole year. By the end of it I was sick of the whole thing. I was sick of myself and sick of writing about myself and I was sick of reading about, watching and thinking about sport.

In January 2020 I attended a joint women's/men's Gaelic football match in Páirc Uí Chaoimh – the first of its kind. The *Irish Examiner* wanted me to write something about the occasion.

After that I decided to take a break from sport. Because of renovations, Ciara and I moved out of our home in Cork city on 2 March to live in a rented house without a television. A great opportunity to live without sport, I thought. Since I began *The First Sunday in September* in 2016 I'd been thinking hard about sport for four years. That was long enough. I also needed some distance from the text of this book. I was busy completing two other books at the time.

I also thought this would be an opportunity to confront my addiction to sport. Time to go into recovery, I thought, and break my habit.

So, that would be that. All the sport coming up in March and April would pass me by. I'd be above it, I wouldn't be 'bovvered' as Lauren says in *The Catherine Tate Show*. And I was interested in how I would feel about this absence, how I would test myself with no football, no rugby, no golf, no cycling, no GAA, no tennis, no Olympics – a whole glorious summer of sport would pass me by and I would blithely enjoy the quiet, reading and writing about other matters. I'd walk in the country, listen to the birds and watch the crops and trees meander through their seasons. I'd read and listen to music in the evenings and at weekends. Maybe go to the odd play or film.

I would also observe myself and my life to see how I could live without sport. If I could live without sport.

And then I would write about that. About the possibility of a life without sport, what such a life would be like.

▲▲▲

My cunning plan failed. Covid-19 hit like a tsunami in March 2020 and shut down sport completely, so that I, along with everybody else, had no choice but to ignore it. It was out of my power to choose. The virus had chosen for me.

And I got on fine without sport in the following months. But sport wasn't really a priority for anyone at that time. Those were the miserable April–May 2020 days of a rising curve, rising ICU pressure, rising nursing-home deaths and job losses; growing fear, with families watching the funerals of loved ones on laptops, sitting around kitchen tables. At a time when we weren't sure we could even beat that bloody curse, let alone when or how or at what cost. My relationship with sport was hardly a priority – or this book, either.

Ironically at that time I actually was living a sporting existence – albeit a type of mirror one. At the time I was busy on a book called *Everything, the Autobiography of Denis Coughlan*. Denis was a famous hurler and footballer for Cork in the 1960s and 1970s and I had been commissioned to co-write his memoir. So, despite my commitment to eschew sport for a while, unlike most other sportspeople, I was actually immersed in it. In the midst of Denis's sporting life I was vicariously winning and losing championship matches with his clubs St Nicholas, Glen Rovers and with Cork.

In those early days of the pandemic, Covid-19 showed us how unimportant sport really is when we compare it to lives lost and existential threats to our well-being and health. Simon Barnes writes about the cancellation of the Ryder Cup in 2001 after 9/11 and how right that was. Sport, at one level, Barnes says is a 'monstrous triviality' in the face of such critical events.

But, during the first Covid-19 lockdown, in retelling Denis's sporting life and the sense of joy and fulfilment that he and his teammates bestowed upon so many (including my teenage self), so often, I was also reminded of the great gift we have in sport.

I was conscious, too, of the sports players, volunteers and administrators who were missing out so badly during the lockdown. All the plans that had been made and all the work for nothing, as event after event was cancelled. All the disappointment of young players who had worked hard to earn their places on teams which had been suddenly shut down. Athletes who had trained for years to perform in events that had been cancelled. All the impacts on people, too – friends and acquaintances among them – who made their living from broadcasting and writing about sport. They lost out and they lost out badly. And how much the fans missed sport – at a time when they probably needed it most – to divert them from the horror the virus was wreaking all around.

In one way the sporting lockdown wasn't significant at all; in another way it was a painful wrench.

During this period there was an orgy of nostalgia about sporting occasions from the past. Since newspapers and broadcasters didn't have any live sport to cover, they replayed and talked about old events, especially the great ones.

On 10 July 2020, when Jack Charlton died, there was a huge outpouring of reminiscence and sadness – he is beloved of Irish people from his football manager days (1986–1996). Jack's death reignited a great wistful reliving of Italia '90, which had taken place thirty years earlier and which was probably Jack's greatest hour as a manager and Ireland's greatest football time. The total immersion into this reliving was perhaps reflective of a longing, not so much to remember better sporting times as better times for the country. How lovely, innocent, joyful, bright and exciting that summer of 1990 was, compared to the dread and grim days of 2020, with Ireland mired in a pandemic, punctuated with daily updates of infections and deaths, instead of updates from the hordes of football fans in Italy and snippets of news about our next game.

While this peak nostalgia didn't surprise me, it didn't tempt me, either. I found I couldn't bring myself to share it. I understood the need to remember and bask in that memory (especially in the Covid-19 summer of 2020) but I was in no way caught up in it. Now, this isn't because I was unmoved by Italia '90 and all that went with it – I was as gripped as anybody else in Ireland at the time.

But – and this is where I seem to part company with many others – for me, once a game is over, it's over. When the championship is lost, it's lost and it's gone. It doesn't really matter that much anymore, its currency is spent and the next championship is far more meaningful. For me, sport is mainly about the moment it's happening. In this, I think it is different from other art forms. In some ways it explains the immediate power and ultra-intensity of sport.

Yes, a great win or a vivid loss leaves ripples on the water and these are felt from time to time – at anniversaries, or when highlights are replayed on TV. I relive some such occasions in this book.

But these are puny compared to the immensity of being in the moment when a great match is in the balance, or even the anticipation of such a moment, as the game with all its import approaches, loaded with possibility.

So I don't feel nostalgic for the ghost of games past. I feel nostalgic for my childhood, with all its innocence and burgeoning hopes. And perhaps that's why I'm not so moved by Italia '90 anymore. By 1990 I was twenty-nine and I no longer dreamed of being a footballer. By then I had been a footballer, however modest.

Andrew O'Hagan talks about the 'present-tenseism' in the social-media universe. People there have a bad relationship with nostalgia because the past to them 'is only nostalgia whereas I think of it as an eternal present'. For me, Italia '90 and many other great sporting events are only nostalgia, but my game when I was twelve kicking a ball around my house is an eternal present. I still live inside it.

When, in June 2020, live sport returned (albeit without fans at games), I was delighted for the thousands of volunteers in clubs up and down the country who give so much to so many and who had been missing the involvement in our communities. I was also delighted for the young players whose lives are so enhanced by sport and who were locked away from their friends and teammates during that time. I was living in a small town in East Cork at the time and the sight of boys and girls cycling to the GAA pitch with hurleys in their backpacks to be with their friends had a heart-warming rightness about it.

We missed all those connections when sport was locked down. And while I was delighted for others when sport returned, I didn't watch any of the live or replayed sport myself. I didn't feel I was missing out. I did tune in to an FA Cup game on my phone one day while I was ironing clothes – it was 20 July. United v Chelsea. But after ten minutes I couldn't listen any more. Not because United were poor (which they were), but because it was too upsetting.

My friend Tom Abernethy had died in March and listening to the match reminded me too much of him. He was the most fervid United fan I have ever known and we had been friends since we were thirteen and had travelled to Old Trafford together when we were seventeen.

During United fixtures we'd text each other; before, during

and after the games. It became a ritual for me, whenever United were playing. It was part of the joy of watching United. But I knew I'd have no text from Tom that day in July and I'd never have another text from him.

I started crying and turned off the match commentary. I finished the ironing and went out for a walk.

My next interaction with sport was unexpected. Ciara and I were on holidays in South Kerry with my brother Padraig, his wife Mags and their son Thomas. The date was the first of August. The holiday home had a TV and Thomas (who was eleven at the time) discovered that the FA Cup Final between Arsenal and Chelsea was being shown.

He asked me to watch the football with him and I agreed, though I'd have preferred to be reading or listening to music.

The game was mesmeric. A lot of people had spoken about how strange and soulless football had become without fans present, but that didn't affect me at all.

On the contrary, without the 'mysterious will of the audience', I found the football more compelling and I could see it more clearly and experience it more purely. I couldn't believe the beauty of the game, the absolute mastery of the players. The complexity of their movements and the clarity of their skills. The immensity of their intellectual capabilities. How they could even imagine, let alone see and make happen their interactions with the ball and each other – how they could communicate so much so quickly. I was sitting there rapt in the game as Thomas played on his Nintendo Switch and Padraig read his *Times*. I was sitting there as rapt as a seven-year-old boy seeing the ineffable beauty of George Best for the first time and the world and time spun silently around me.

In the opening moments of the game, the Arsenal full back, Kieran Tierney, clips the ball high down the left wing. The accuracy of this pass is incredible. Inches to the left and it will go out of play, inches to the right and the Chelsea full back will be under it. The ball travels fifty metres through the air and it is perfect in accuracy and pace and height – a three-dimensional miracle. Can you imagine how difficult this is? This is the equivalent of what Yo-Yo Ma is doing with his cello, or Frida Kahlo with her brush, but Tierney has to do it under pressure with milliseconds to spare, in a high-stakes game. And he has to imagine it first. He has to conceive of this perfect pass, like Michelangelo conceived of the Pietà emerging from the marble.

Then he has to execute it.

The act is partly instinctive and partly as a result of countless brain functions spilling countless neurons through his premotor cortex, passing countless messages through his brain and down his spine to his left foot. His left foot receives these signals and translates them into an action so pure and so perfect as to render it virtually impossible.

And this magic isn't even remarked upon by the commentator. Why would it, when it is replicated minute by minute by the other twenty-one players on the pitch and the thousands of other top-level footballers week-in week-out in leagues around the world? But it is remarkable, it is breathtaking. Once, I might have been able to create such magic, and I created a version of this magic around my house when I was twelve.

And (through the artifice of sport) I can still experience performing this magic as my brain floods mirror neurons through my body, creating the intersubjectivity I talked about earlier. I knew, even as I was feeling the incredible beauty of Kieran Tierney and all the Kieran Tierneys in that game, that a kind of biological mimesis was happening inside my body, but it didn't diminish the experience one iota.

I never thought I could be so moved again by play, but it happened that day in August 2020. In my self-imposed sporting abstinence, during a game I had chanced upon, the result of which I couldn't have cared less about.

The ball flies down the wing into the faultless path of Ainsley Maitland-Niles, who – just as easily – changes direction and pace to mirror the ball. He had begun his run down the line (being careful not to be offside before the ball was delivered) moments before the pass. His body is both flesh and not. It's the idea of flesh but it's more the idea than the reality.

He has waited just the right number of moments, his run is perfectly timed – and this takes a level of intellectual ability beyond the best quantum physicists. The ball bounces to his left but he knows its spin will take it into his stride. He continues to run, the ball bouncing high beside him. He is running flat out now and jostling with the Chelsea full back, César Azpilicueta, but his first touch of the ball, with his head, is purposeful and powerful. He had planned it only milliseconds before but that's all the time he needs to perform multifaceted physical actions, controlling the ball and accomplishing a myriad of related functions.

The ball travels another twenty metres under this impetus, utterly accurately again, right into Maitland-Niles's path, exactly as he had planned. Just as he is about to reach it, running full pelt, Azpilicueta pushes him in the back – this too is perfectly timed (Azpilicueta's intelligence is also of the highest order and the defender knows exactly what Maitland-Niles is trying to do). He times the nudge milliseconds before Maitland-Niles intends to touch the ball forward with his right foot, but the Arsenal player can adjust his body and the momentum of his toe sufficiently to counteract the impact of the push and perfectly control the ball and take it to where it needs to be next and where he intends to be with it. He's like a great chess grandmaster planning four moves ahead, but he's doing it hundreds of times more quickly.

The ball is Maitland-Niles's principle of intention, remember, but it has – at the same time – possessed his body as its object. It needs to be right on the white sideline of the pitch and so it is. It is now running outside the line, but it directs Maitland-Niles to touch it again, with more force because he has suddenly accelerated beforehand, to take him beyond Azpilicueta. The pace of the ball has to also be sufficiently increased – in another mirroring – so he doesn't overrun it or have created insufficient distance between himself and the defender. But now the end-line is approaching fast and the ball is going to go out of play for a Chelsea goal kick.

At the same time that Maitland-Niles is calculating impossible mathematical equations of time and space (in three dimensions), Azpilicueta is performing his own computational wonders. He has to foresee what Maitland-Niles will do before the Arsenal player knows he is going to do it. And he has to take into account several interlocking possibilities depending on what will happen. But the defender is capable of achieving this – his intellectual abilities are also beyond imagining.

The ball doesn't go out of play. Just as it is crossing the line, with Azpilicueta hovering, Maitland-Niles somehow (I don't know how, even though I watched it closely and have re-watched it dozens of times since) spins through space – he's suspended there like air itself – and he skips his right foot over the ball and turns his body and reverses his momentum and swivels his hips and flicks the ball with the inside of his left foot (stopping it) and at the same time he halts his own body into stillness.

As Maitland-Niles is spinning through Wembley Stadium space, through the sacred, unreal time of *kairos*, the Earth is spinning beneath him and around our sun. All the Earth's sister planets and other dwarf planets and dozens of moons and millions of asteroids, comets and meteoroids are spinning, too. Our solar system is spinning through the galaxy as are all the other solar systems, and we are all, suddenly very small. I am tinier than a mote of dust and it's wonderful to be so inconsequential.

Maitland-Niles (back on Earth, near the corner flag) is now completely immobile but his body contains the tensile power of immediate and devastating movement – should he need it again. Now he is facing the goal, and the ball is completely stationary and perfectly placed for him to rotate his hips (all this is in the same movement, these are not separate movements, all this happens at the same time – though in that movement time is meaningless, the imaginings of a child, the meanderings of an old man).

He skips twice to measure his next touch and create uncertainty in the full back, and he flicks the ball with the outside of his right foot – just a couple of inches, but that's all he needs – and while he's doing that he also lifts his head (for the tiniest moment) and he looks towards the goal and sees his teammate Pierre-Emerick Aubemeyang at the near post. And Ainsley Maitland-Niles – impossible genius, ethereal being – strikes the ball forcefully, powering it thirty metres, at pace, at the perfect height, right onto Aubemeyang's head.

Now, this very incomplete description, of an insignificant play, early in the game, involving four players, takes place – in real time – over a period of ten seconds. All this happened in ten seconds. And there are 540 times ten seconds in a football match. And what you've just read is a description of the actions of only four players, not taking into account the other eighteen. And it didn't take into account what Kieran Tierney did after he delivered the ball down the line, or what Pierre-Emerick Aubemeyang did to get to that near post, or the complex series of movements that César Azpilicueta undertook to limit the damage to his team.

I've described those ten seconds with 1,200 words, but I could have done it in 2,000 words and it would still be incomplete. Were I to describe another 539 such moves in such detail – the full game – that would take over a million words. That's about thirteen times the size of this book. And that's the actions in one game out of thousands of games, in one sport out of dozens of sports, in one season out of maybe seventy seasons in one sports fan's life.

So, when Joyce Carol Oates described boxing as something profound happening in a place beyond words, it's because sport cannot be sufficiently described by words – it would take forests of trees to provide the paper for the words to be written on. She also points out that, in sport, 'so much happens so swiftly and with such heart-stopping subtlety that you cannot absorb it'. For some reason (and I don't know what it is), in the 2020 FA Cup Final, I was able to absorb it, but not in a way that words can describe. Words are insufficient.

All the 'punditry' (I can't bring myself to treat that as a real word) and all the sports writing and all the commentary and analysis and replaying, and all the social media posts and all the post-mortems of fans, down all the years – all of it combined – can't come remotely close to what's really happening in the real time (in the *kairos* or unreal time) of games. What has been dreamed up and created by the incalculable genius of sportspeople.

After that I didn't watch much sport or engage with it for a while. But then my nephew, Colm Coakley, was picked to play in a championship hurling match for his club Erins Own against Newtownshandrum.

Colm had been away in Australia for a couple of years and he wasn't expecting to play Senior hurling again, but the club realised they needed him to do a job for the team at centre field, even though he was now thirty-five. Colm is a physiotherapist and I had been attending him in his clinic that month in Cork city with a back problem. So there was a fair bit of chatting about his own fitness (after a hamstring pull) and the game. Because of Covid-19 no fans were allowed to attend the match, so Ciara and I watched it being streamed in the house in Dunmanway where we were living at the time.

I was shocked at my reaction to the game. There was none of the FA Cup Final intellectual appreciation of the skill and intelligence of the players. Instead there was pure emotion, the craving for Colm and his team to win. The excitement and *ekstasis* of the moment when I saw Con Roche score a goal when I was ten and all the other such moments I've described earlier.

I found myself shouting at the iPad, shouting at the referee, shouting at the players and bellowing when Colm scored a goal in the last minute of the game to win it. My heart was pounding, my reason was absent. Ciara had to calm me down.

I was so far inside the game and at such a passionate pitch that it was a wrench when the game was over and I had to leave it and return to the ordinary time of *chronos*.

I immediately phoned my brother Dermot (Colm's father) to prolong and share the moment with him. I didn't have to think twice, I just picked up the phone and rang him. I had to. My need for connection in the moment was impossible to deny.

I could hear immediately that Dermot, too, was high, and only coming out of *kairos*. We talked about the game and the great win. We didn't have much to add to what had happened, it was only necessary to share it, to bond, to stretch it out for another while.

Afterwards I reflected on the game and my reaction. I realised that my compulsion to phone Dermot was the same one that had compelled me (when I was ten after Dermot had won an All-Ireland) to run out of my house to meet my friend Paul Redmond and share the moment with him.

In the way that I shared Medinah with Jack and my mother, and Ollie Ryan shared '99 with his father, and Simon Critchley shared a Merseyside derby win with his father, and in the way those Waterford people shared the Munster Hurling Championship with their loved ones in St Otteran's Cemetery in June 2002.

In the way that my father shared my Minor hurling All-Ireland win with me, when he kissed me on the platform of Kent Station.

Covid-19 had changed everything and it had changed nothing.

I am different after this book, but my immersion in sport is exactly the same.

And so, I had returned. My 2020 coronavirus comeback was complete. Sport had drawn me back in. Its gravitational force had been too strong and my willingness to comply with its sweet old pull had been too ready.

I don't think I'll be resisting sport again. What would be the point?

PART 7

RETURNING HOME

TO INNOCENCE

The pages that follow are dedicated to the children who once upon a time, years ago, crossed my path on Calella de la Costa. They had been playing football and were singing: We lost, we won, either way we had fun.

– *Football in Sun and Shadow*, Eduardo Galeano

THERE ARE SIX STAGES OF MY sporting life. Five are over and now I'm in the final stage.

The first was in my pre-teens. When I was initiated to sport and it was a kind of wonder to me. When I was innocent and I played on my own or with family or friends with joy and for joy and to be playing. To play was to be alive then and when I was kicking my ball around my home, the rightness of it was never in doubt.

The second phase was when I went to boarding school at the age of twelve. There I began to play sport seriously. Sport had a significance in St Colman's College, Fermoy; it was a valuable form of currency. When I say sport, I mean hurling. I craved that currency and I played and trained and put myself forward. I wanted to belong on those teams even though I learned a hard lesson in my teenage years in that school. I learned that I was alone – and more, that we are all, essentially, alone. My childhood dreams of togetherness and family were unravelled every third Sunday night when I was driven to Fermoy – away from everything I loved – to that cold and ruthless place. This was life, it was survive or be crushed. It was do or die. It was win or lose. I would never be the same again, but I guess it's like that for most people: growing up means to separate the ideal from the actual. It means a loss of innocence – the place where play comes from. My childhood game was replaced by real, organised sport: team games where you compete against others in public and where you win or lose.

The third phase of my sporting life was when I was in college. It was not a good time for me. I struggled with the isolation and the knowledge of being alone. I was doing the wrong course in UCC. But I couldn't gather the strength or belief that there was a right course. I wouldn't (as Ciara's father, Kevin, used to say) lead nor drive. I was stuck. During those years I played my best hurling and I played Minor and Under 21 championship hurling for Cork as well as for UCC in the Fitzgibbon Cup. I also played my best football for Mallow United and loved every moment of it. I played hurling for my GAA club, Mallow, too. In a way, at that time, sport was my tether – the 'fine thread', as Jean-Philippe Toussaint put it, connecting me to the world.

Without it, without its reality and purpose, I'm not sure what would have happened to me.

Then, in my mid-twenties, I met Ciara and I felt a purpose, I sensed a future for myself. I got a job and had something to get up for in the morning. I didn't need sport as much, in this my fourth stage as a sportsman, but I still loved it during my last playing days in football and hurling – hurling especially, which I played for my beloved club until I was thirty. I wanted to be part of the collective, but I was also drawing away from my hometown. I was living in Cork and I was being pulled towards my future there. In *Minor Monuments* Ian Maleney describes how, in his twenties, the direction of his life had led him away from the people who had formed him and the places he had known and loved the longest. He was being true to himself when he had to leave home to find what he could only find elsewhere. This was true for me, too. Also, since my body was rebelling against the years of training and effort, staying fit was becoming more and more difficult. I could no longer be a hurler.

But I could be a golfer, the game for all those no longer able to (or willing to) run around. Golf gives the companionship, the concentration, the distraction and the competitive urge that 'real' sports give. But you can do it while you're getting old and fat and infirm, like me. Golf was the fifth stage of my sporting life and I still play the odd round, though I'm no longer in a club or have a handicap. I play for fun, not to compete. I play to remember the joy of hitting a ball well, of being in flight. I play golf to remember when I could play football and hurling, too, and when things I did on pitches set other hearts racing. When I broke my collarbone I quit golf for a while, and cancelled my membership of Mallow Golf Club. My clubs spend over 99.9

per cent of their time in the shed these days and almost none of their time in the boot of the car or on the golf course. I play in my mind at night when sleep won't come. And when I do play a round or two a year with friends and family, I feel good. Ciara always says I should play more and I do try.

The sixth and final stage of my sporting life is as a fan. This is where most people who engage with sport are located. They are on the populated side of the street, as Tom McIntyre put it, and they are happy there. Some, like me, used to play but can no longer tog out. Some didn't but they still had their own initiations and their moments of glory – when they wept for joy, for club or county or family. At least I hope they did, everybody deserves to know that bliss.

Of course I was a fan of sport since that moment in 1971 when I saw Con Roche score that goal for Cork from a sideline cut and I have been since. Players are fans, too. Their inner children's hearts quicken at the sight of the beloved jersey and the *agôn* unfolding. I mostly watch hurling, football, rugby and golf, but I'll watch almost anything sporting – cycling is great and tennis, too. I'm working on my addiction, as I've said, but not too seriously. Give me chastity and continence, Lord, but not yet, as the patron saint of professional footballers once said.

How lucky I am to live in a world where men and women like George Best and Con Roche are possible and to have felt the wonder they induce. How happy I am to have known such people, to have played with and against them and to have witnessed them up close and far away in all their universal glory. In all their unadorned beauty.

I rejoice in this and I give thanks for it.

I've been playing and watching games for over fifty years, now, but of all the games I've seen and played, the one that gives me the greatest joy was when, in my innocence, I kicked my ball around my home on the Cork Road in Mallow. The big winning and losing moments, the ladders and table by-products of the industry (as Fay Zwicky called them) don't engage me – have never engaged me – as purely as that game engages me.

When I played to play and not to win – this is the sporting memory I hold most dear. It's no coincidence that I can remember that game with more intensity of detail than any other I've ever experienced. One of the first games of my life, when I was a child.

We remember what is most significant to us. So it's no surprise that all the play which has fired my imagination is rooted in and has sprung out of the place where I was born and raised by my mother and father alongside my sisters and brothers.

Tom Kilroy talks about the tactile nature of memory, of how we can reach out and touch the remembered surfaces of the past. I can touch the remembered surfaces of my childhood home, my childhood game.

The rough pebble-dash of the house wall.

The stippled concrete on the pillar.

The jagged mineral felt on the roof of Faust's kennel.

The scratchy straw on the bed of the kennel.

The tiny dimples on my ball.

The uneven bark of the cypress trees.

I touch them all, I touch them now,

As I place the ball upon the ground

And begin my game again.

ACKNOWLEDGEMENTS

I want to thank you, the reader, for taking the time to read this, I hope you liked it.

I want to thank all the people I have played with or against in sport. It's been great. I love you all.

A special thanks to all the volunteers – who have done so much for me and for others – in my clubs: Mallow GAA, Mallow United AFC, Mallow Golf Club, my school, St Colman's College Fermoy, my college, University College Cork, and for Cork teams on which I played. Thanks to everyone who supported me during my playing days.

Love and thanks always to Ciara, my wonderful wife, and my wonderful family, all three generations. I'm thinking of my brothers and sisters especially, who have done so much for me and who have looked after me all my life: Mary, Dermot, John, Úna, Cathy, Padraig and Pauline.

I dedicate this to my mother and father, through whose unfailing love and support I had so many wonderful opportunities in life, including sport. I miss them deeply and will love them always. I dedicate it to Roisín and Jack, too, the children I never had.

Huge thanks to all at Merrion Press especially to Patrick O'Donoghue who believed in this book from the start. Thanks so much also to Conor Graham, Maeve Convery, Wendy Logue, Sarah Doyle and Peter O'Connell. Thanks so much to Djinn von Noorden, who copy-edited this book so brilliantly. Thanks to Fiachra McCarthy for the wonderful cover design.

My sports essay 'Five Moments in Sport', which appears here in a different form, was published by *The Stinging Fly* in 2019. Thanks to Danny Denton and Declan Meade for that.

The same essay subsequently was published in *The Holly Bough*. Thanks to John Dolan for that.

The essay 'Hurt 1: Masculinity' was first published by *The42* in 2020 as part of their *Bylines* series. Thanks to Adrian Russell for that.

The essay 'Possession' was published by *The Winter Papers* in 2021. Thanks to Kevin Barry and Olivia Smith for that.

The essay 'A Place Beyond Words' was published by *Aethlon: the Journal of Sport Literature* in 2022. Thanks to Michele Schiavone and the Sports Literature Association for that.

Other pieces of sports writing published in the *Irish Examiner* also appear in this book, including 'Hurling is in the Quiet'. Thanks to Tony Leen, Colm O'Connor and Larry Ryan for that.

Some of this book was developed in workshops led by Sinéad Gleeson (West Cork Literary Festival) and Arnold Fanning (*The Stinging Fly*), thanks to Sinéad and Arnold and all my fellow participants in those. Most of this book was critiqued in my two writing groups, by Arnold Fanning, Rachel Andrews, Madeleine D'Arcy, Eileen O'Donoghue, Anna Foley and Diarmuid Hickey; big thanks to them all. Thanks also to Anna Foley, Mary Morrissy, Tony Hegarty and my brother Dermot Coakley who read this book and critiqued it. Thanks to Dermot for the brilliant cover photo. Thanks to Tony for allowing me to include his story. Thanks also to Mike (Rusty) Russell for allowing me to include his story. Big thanks to Noel O'Regan for his close reading of the text, his great suggestions and his support. Thanks to my brother John Coakley who translated some of *Le Football, une peste émotionelle: la barbarie des stages* for me.

Thanks to Pádraig J. Daly for kindly allowing the use of his poem 'Footballer', which first appeared in his collection *The Voice of the Hare*. Thanks also to Dedalus Press (www.dedaluspress.com), its publisher.

ACKNOWLEDGEMENTS

Thanks to my fellow-travellers in sport: Barry Roche, Martin O'Donovan and David Coleman. Long time, good times.

Huge thanks to all the people out there who supported me in my writing; who facilitated my publications; who edited, workshopped, reviewed, taught and critiqued me; who gave me cover quotes (especially Catherine Kirwan, who kindly gave me a quote for *Whatever It Takes*); who encouraged me and sent me kind words. I'm so grateful. Here's a long list of names; if you're not there, it doesn't mean I don't appreciate your support. I have so many people to thank, for so many reasons. I am very grateful to everyone.

Tom Abernethy (RIP), Tony 'Tucker' Allen (RIP), Dan Beechinor (RIP), John Breen, Marjorie Brennan, Fiona Byrne, Malachy Clerkin, Tommy Conroy (RIP), Gavin Cooney, Sean Cooney (RIP), Emily Cooper, Canon Jackie Corkery (RIP), Eugene Cosgrove, Patrick Cotter, Christy Coughlan (RIP), Denis Coughlan, Shane Cronin, John Crowley, Kieran Cunningham, Tadhg Curtis, Gráinne Daly, Martin Doyle, Ali Driscoll, Adrian Duncan, Nicky English, Wendy Erskine, Tanya Farrelly, Mary Feehan, John Grainger, Dave Hannigan, Joe Hayes (RIP), Liam Hayes, Molly Hennigan, Rónán Hession, Liam Heylin, Vincent Hogan, Paul Howard, Denis Hurley, Claire Keegan, Mark Kelleher, Patricia Looney, Tim MacGabhann, Derry Mannix, Jordan McCarthy, Thomas McCarthy, Enda McEvoy, Lisa McInerney, Declan Meade, Thomas Morris, Michael Moynihan, Dr Con Murphy, Steve Murphy, Archdeacon Michael O'Brien (RIP), Manus O'Callaghan, John O'Connell, Gavin O'Connor, Paul O'Connor (RIP), Eddie O'Donnell, Gary O'Donovan, Sharon O'Donovan, Eimear O'Herlihy, Kate Phelan, Deirdre Roberts, Donal Ryan, Eimear Ryan, Ollie Ryan (RIP), Michele Schiavone, Gus Sexton, Kieran Shannon, Percy Shannon (RIP), Liam Sheehan, Ronan Sheehan, Eamonn Sheehy, Canon Bertie Troy (RIP), Eibhear Walshe, Michelle Walshe, Adrian Wisreich, Mary White, John Whyte (RIP).

FURTHER READING

Martin Alsiö, *The Hooligans' Death List: A global search for accountability between accidents and intentions.* idrottsforum.org, 2013.

Nadia Bailey, 'Pas de Quatre, an essay' in *Balancing Acts: Women in Sport: Essays on power, performance, bodies and love.* Justin Wolfers and Erin Riley (eds), Brow Books, 2018.

John Bale, *Landscapes of Modern Sport.* Leicester University Press, 1994.

Simon Barnes, *The Meaning of Sport.* Short Books, 2006.

Simon Barnes, *Losing it: A Lifetime in Pursuit of Sporting Excellence.* Bloomsbury Sport, 2016.

BBC, *State of Sport 2018: Half of retired sportspeople have concerns over mental and emotional wellbeing.* BBC, 2018.

Dominique Bodin, Gaelle Sempé, Luc Robène and Stéphane Héas, 'Ethics and Sport in Europe' in *Ethics and Sport in Europe,* Dominique Bodin and Gaelle Sempé (eds). Council of Europe, 2011.

Jean-Marie Brohm, *Sport: A Prison of Measured Time: Essays,* translated by Ian Fraser. Ink Links, 1978.

Jean-Marie Brohm, Marc Perelman, *Le Football, une peste émotionelle: la barbarie des stages.* Gallimard, 2006.

Denis M. Brown, *The Toxic Masculinity Crisis.* CreateSpace Independent Publishing Platform, 2018.

Michael L. Butterworth, and Stormi D. Moskal, 'American Football, Flags, and "Fun": The Bell Helicopter Armed Forces Bowl and the Rhetorical Production of Militarism' in *Communication, Culture & Critique* 2:4 (2009).

Roger Caillois, *Man, Play and Games.* Urbana, 2011.

Richard Carew, *The Survey of Cornwall.* London, 1602.

Meghan Casserly, 'Sex And The Super Bowl: Indianapolis Puts Spotlight On Teen Sex Trafficking'. Forbes.com, 2012.

Noam Chomsky, *Noam Chomsky on Sports.* YouTube, 2015.

Galen Clavio and Andrea N. Eagleman, 'Gender and Sexually Suggestive Images in Sports Blogs'. *Journal of Sport Management,* 2011.

Jay Coakley, *Sports in Society: Issues and Controversies.* McGraw Hill, 2016.

Paula Cocozza, 'Ross Raisin: "Football doesn't fit neatly inside the label of literary fiction"'. *The Guardian,* 2017.

Steven Connor, *A Philosophy of Sport.* Reaktion Books, 2011.

Gavin Cooney, *Behind the Lines Podcast.* The42, 2019–.

Simon Critchley, *What We Think About When We Think About Football.* Profile Books, 2017.

Kieran Cunningham, 'Why is the Impact of the GAA Ignored by so many Irish Writers and Artists?' Buzz.ie, 2017.

Gráinne Daly, *Ireland of Sports and Scholars: Sport and sporting sites in the Irish Literature.* Sports Literature Association Conference, 23 June 2021.

Joan Didion, 'Why I Write'. *The New York Times*, 1976.

Annie Dillard, *The Writing Life*. Harper Perennial, 1989.

Annie Dillard, *An American Childhood*. Harper Collins, 2013.

Adrian Duncan, *Midfield Dynamo*. The Lilliput Press, 2021.

Ciarán Dunne, 'An examination of the photographic coverage of sportswomen in the Irish print media: a study of an Irish broadsheet newspaper'. *Sport in Society*, 2017.

Paul Durcan, 'The Beautiful Game', *Life is a Dream: 40 Years Reading Poems*. Harvill Secker, 2009.

Andrew Edgar, *Sport and Art: An Essay in the Hermeneutics of Sport*. Taylor and Francis, 2013.

Wendy Erskine, 'OK, son?'. *The Demented Goddess*, 2019.

Wendy Erskine and Danny Denton, podcast: 'Wendy Erskine Reads Adrian Duncan'. *The Stinging Fly*, 2019.

Ray Fair, *The steep economic cost of contact sports injuries*. Pbs.org, 2017.

Franklin Foer, *How Soccer Explains the World: An Unlikely Theory of Globalization*. Harper Perennial, 2005.

Pierre-Henry Frangne, 'Philosophy, ethics and sport' in *Ethics and Sport in Europe*, Dominique Bodin and Gaelle Sempé (eds). Council of Europe. 2011.

Eduardo Galeano, *Football in Sun and Shadow: An Emotional History of World Cup Football*. Fourth Estate, 1997.

Adam Gopnik, *Paris to the Moon*. Random House, 2000.

Frédéric Gros, *A Philosophy of Walking*. Verso, 2015.

Elizabeth Grosz, *Volatile Bodies: Toward a Corporeal Feminism (Theories of Representation and Difference)*. Indiana University Press, 1994.

Charlotte Guest, 'The Thing About Sport and Poetry Is That They're Kind of Similar' in *Balancing Acts: Women in Sport: Essays on power, performance, bodies and love*. Justin Wolfers and Erin Riley (eds), Brow Books, 2018.

Dave Hannigan, 'How the power of sport can help Alzheimer's and dementia patients'. *The Irish Times*, 2019.

Johan Huizinga, *Homo Ludens: A study of the Play Element in Culture*. The Beacon Press, 1950.

Joe Humphreys, *Foul Play: What's Wrong with Sport*. Icon Books, 2008.

Siri Hustvedt, *Living, Thinking, Looking*. Sceptre, 2013.

Kalle Jonasson, '"Sport qua science": Michel Serres' ball as an asset of knowledge', *Sport in Society, Cultures, Commerce, Media, Politics*, 2019.

Mary Jo Kane, 'Sex Sells Sex, Not Women's Sports: So what does sell women's sports?'. *The Nation*, 2011.

John B. Keane, *The Man From Clare*. Father Mathew Hall, 1962.

Karen Kedmey, *How to Be an Artist, According to Louise Bourgeois*. Artsy.net, 2017.

Thomas Kilroy, *Over the Backyard Wall*. The Lilliput Press, 2018.

Karl Ove Knausgaard and Fredrik Ekelund, *Home and Away: Writing the Beautiful Game.* Vintage, 2016.

Anna Krien, *Night Games: A Journey to the Dark Side of Sport.* Yellow Jersey, 2016.

Simon Kuper, *Football Against the Enemy.* Orion, 1994.

Olivia Laing, *Strange Weather: Art in an Emergency.* Picador, 2020.

Jessica Luther and Kavitha Davidson, *Loving Sports When They Don't Love You Back: Dilemmas of the Modern Fan.* University of Texas Press, 2020.

Helen Macdonald, *H is for Hawk.* Jonathan Cape, 2014.

Norman Mailer, *The Fight.* Little, Brown & Co, 1975.

Ian Maleney, *Minor Monuments.* Tramp Press, 2019.

Everett Dean Martin, *The Behavior of Crowds: A Psychological Study.* Harper and Brothers, 1920.

John McAuliffe, *Everything to Play For: 99 Poems about Sport.* Poetry Ireland, 2015.

Thomas Page McBee, *Amateur.* Canongate, 2019.

Damian McCarney, '[Tom McIntyre] Still embracing the ghost'. *The Anglo Celt,* 2013.

John McGahern, 'Love of the World' in *Granta: The Magazine of New Writing* (Autumn 1997).

John McGahern, *Memoir.* Faber, 2005.

National Gambling Impact Study Commission, *Final Report.* NGISC, 1999.

Joyce Carol Oates, *On Boxing.* Dolphin/Doubleday, 1987.

Seán Ó Faoláin, 'The End of a Good Man', in David Marcus (ed.), *Irish Sporting Short Stories.* Appletree Press, 1995.

George Orwell, 'The Sporting Spirit', *Tribune,* 1945.

Fintan O'Toole, 'The truth according to Brian Friel', *The Irish Times,* 2015.

Fintan O'Toole, 'Let's abolish culture and call it sport', *The Irish Times,* 2019.

David Papineau, *Knowing the Score: How Sport Teaches us about Philosophy (and Philosophy about Sport).* Constable, 2017.

Pete Pattisson and Roshan Sedhai, 'Sudden deaths of hundreds of migrant workers in Qatar not investigated', *The Guardian,* 2019.

Georges Perec, *W, or the Memory of Childhood,* translated by David Bellos. Harvill, 1988.

Ross Raisin, *A Natural.* Jonathan Cape, 2017.

Sally Rooney, 'On my radar: Sally Rooney's cultural highlights', *The Guardian,* 2017.

Caitlin Roper, 'Naked women in Sports Illustrated isn't about giving them a voice', *The Sydney Morning Herald,* 2018.

Eimear Ryan, 'The Fear of Winning' in *Winter Papers,* 2016 and *The Irish Examiner,* 2017.

Richie Sadlier, *Recovering.* Gill Books, 2019.

George Saunders, 'Who are all these Trump supporters? At the candidate's rallies, a new understanding of America emerges', *The New Yorker,* 2016.

Jonathan W. Schooler and Tonya Engstler-Schooler, 'Verbal overshadowing of visual memories:

Some things are better left unsaid', *Cognitive Psychology*, 1990.

John Self, 'Andrew O'Hagan: "The great chip pan fire novelist of the age"', *The Irish Times*, 2020.

Michel Serres, *The Parasite*, translated by Lawrence R. Schehr. University of Minnesota Press, 2007.

Julie Shaw, *The Memory Illusion: Remembering, Forgetting, and the Science of False Memory*. Random House Books, 2017.

Jaime Shultz, *Women's Sports: what everyone needs to know*. Oxford University Press, 2018.

Rebecca Slater, 'A Coach's Hands, A Woman's Body: The Sexualised Relationship Between Male Supervisors and Female Athletes' in *Balancing Acts: Women in Sport: Essays on power, performance, bodies and love*. Justin Wolfers and Erin Riley (eds), Brow Books, 2018.

Ed Smith, *What Sport Tells Us About Life*. Penguin, 2008.

Rebecca Solnit, *Wanderlust: A History of Walking*. Verso Books, 2001.

Sport Ireland, *Irish Sports Monitor Annual Report 2019*. Sport Ireland, 2020.

Erin Stewart, 'Tennis, Outer Space & Breastfeeding in Public: the Surprising Relationship between Sports & Feminism' in *Balancing Acts: Women in Sport: Essays on power, performance, bodies and love*.

Justin Wolfers and Erin Riley (eds), Brow Books, 2018.

Jean-Philippe Toussaint, *Football*. Fitzcarraldo, 2016.

Peter Pericles Trifonas, *Umberto Eco and Football*. Icon Books, 2001.

Toko-pa Turner, *Belonging: Remembering Ourselves Home*. Her Own Room Press, 2018.

Robert J. Vallerand et al., 'On passion and sports fans: A look at football', *Journal of Sports Science*, 2008.

James S. Vass Jr, *Cheering For Self: An Ethnography of the Basketball Event*. iUniverse, 2003.

L.S. Vygotsky, *Thought and Language*. MIT Press, 1986.

David Foster Wallace, *Both Flesh and Not: Essays*. Hamish Hamilton, 2012.

Deb Waterhouse-Watson, *Athletes, Sexual Assault and Trials by Media: Narrative Immunity*. Taylor and Francis, 2013.

Jonathan Wilson, 'The candystripe passions of grandfather, father and son'. SAFC Blog, 2011.

D.W. Winnicott, *Playing and Reality*. Routledge, 1971.

Justin Wolfers and Erin Riley (eds), *Balancing Acts: Women in Sport: Essays on power, performance, bodies and love*. Brow Books, 2018.

Fay Zwicky, 'Border Crossings' from *The Collected Poems of Fay Zwicky*. UWA Publishing, 2017.